EVERYDAY SOUTHERN
COMFORTS

by Steven Baker

TABLE OF CONTENTS

INTRODUCTION 04
INSPIRATION 08
APPETIZERS 09
    Pimento Cheese .10
    Lady Fingers 11
    Nacho Cheese Dip 12
    Guacamole 12
    Fried Green Tomatoes 13
    Bacon Wrapped Chicken Bites 14
    Roasted Pecans .14
    Sweet Potato Rice Lettuce Wraps 15
    Coconut Shrimp with Spicy Aioli 16
    Pennies From Heaven 17
    Pizza Pockets 18
SOUPS & SALADS 20
    Hamburger Soup .21
    Potato & Sausage Soup 22
    Turkey Chili 24
    Broccoli Almond Salad 26
    Chicken & Rice Soup 27
    Chickpea Jar Salad 28
    Watergate Salad 28
    Chicken & Vegetable Soup 29
    Butternut Squash Soup 30
BREADS 32
    Sweet Potato Biscuits 33
    Skillet Cornbread 34
    Buttermilk Biscuits 36
    Granddaddy's Southern Biscuits 37
    Rustic Dutch Oven Bread 38
    Hoecakes 40
    Dinner Rolls 41
    Blueberry Muffins 42

SUPPERS 44
    Hamburgers & Gravy 45
    Fried Chicken 46
    Sunday Night Pot Roast 48
    Cheesy Shells with Meat Sauce 50
    Chickens on the Grill 52
    BBQ Ribs 53
    Adult Mac & Cheese 54
    Pan Seared Scallops 56
    Make Ahead Turkey Lasagna 57
    Beef Stew 58
    Sweet & Spicy
    Grilled Chicken Breast with Pinea 60
    Chicken Casserole 61
    Cider Beer Roasted Chicken 62
    Linguine with Roasted Shrimp
    & Cream Sauce 64
    Stuffed Bell Pepper Casserole 65
    Roasted Turkey & Gravy 66
    Baked Salmon Fillets with Toasted Panko . . . 68
    Moroccan Risotto 69
    Roasted Peppers
    Stuffed with Cauliflower Rice 70
    New Orleans Style Gumbo 72

TABLE OF CONTENTS

SIDES 74
    Broccoli Casserole. 75
    Roasted Butternut Squash & Carrots. 76
    Corn off the Cob. 78
    Sweet Potato Crunch. 79
    Grilled Bacon Wrapped Asparagus 80
    Herb Roasted Potatoes. 81
    Mexican Rice 82
    Cauliflower Fried Rice. 84
    Classic Thanksgiving Dressing. 85
    Potato Salad. 86
    Marinated Carrots. 86
    Navy Beans 87
    Scalloped Potatoes 88
    Mashed Potatoes 88
    French Fries 89

DESSERTS 90
    Banana Pudding. 91
    Cheesecake. 92
    Pie Crust Dough 94
    Chocolate Pie. 95
    Lemon Pound Cake 96
    Pumpkin Cheesecake 97
    Old Fashioned Butter Cake
    with Chocolate Icing 98
    Mama Lou's Butterscotch Pie. 100
    Sweet Potato Pie 102
    Brownies 103
    Carrot Cake 104
    Pecan Pie. 106
    Caramel Sauce. 107
    Kentucky Bourbon Cake w/Caramel Drizzle . 108
    Pumpkin Oatmeal Cookies 109
    Chocolate Soufflé 110

THIS & THAT 111
    BBQ Sauce. 112
    Cane & Herb Dressing 113
    Spicy Honey Mustard. 113
    Strawberry Vinaigrette. 114
    Creamy Greek Yogurt Dressing 114
    Classic Margarita 115
    Orangeade 115
    Pitcher of Margaritas (for Cheaters) 116
    Simple Syrup 116
    Grown-Up Lemonade. 117
    Mojito 117
    Marinara Sauce 118
    Sticky & Sweet Bourbon Sauce. 119
    Kitchen Conversions 120

INTRODUCTION

INTRODUCTION

I was born and raised in eastern North Carolina, and if there's one thing about us southerners, it's that we know our food. We've perfected dishes that have been handed down from generation to generation. Cooking has been a love of mine for as long as I can remember. Standing in the kitchen for hours preparing meals may seem like a chore to some people, but for me it's my escape from this crazy world.

My love for cooking started when I was just a kid. I would love nothing better than to help out in the kitchen by stirring this or adding that. My grandmother would keep my sister and I after school and in the summer, and my favorite thing to do with her would be to cook. I was fascinated by just watching her do her thing. I didn't even have to help; just watching was good enough for me.

Watching my parents and grand-parents in the kitchen, I wanted to make my own food, something that I could call my own. My first recipe was a hot dog sandwich. It was two pieces of toasted bread with a hot dog, ketchup, and mustard in the middle. Groundbreaking right!

As I got older and had more freedom in the kitchen, I started to cook things like boxed dinners and easy recipes such as spaghetti or baked chicken. I thought I was really something then!

It wasn't until I was in my 20's and I was home recovering from a major surgery that my mind was truly blown. I couldn't do anything but sit around and watch TV all day, and it was then that I discovered a little thing called Food Network. I would watch hours upon hours and episode after episode of cooking shows while sitting there taking notes like a student. I learned all about cooking with fresh herbs, the essentials of baking, how to dice an onion, making things from scratch, and knife skills.

It was then that I started to experiment with food. I would take things that I already knew how to cook and change them up to boost the flavor. I also tried my hand at dishes that were completely new, strange, and frankly scary. I had some hits and misses and I even caught my oven on fire once or twice.

The first real recipe that I conjured up was my cheesecake recipe. It was a big hit with my family and friends. I even started baking them for my friend's local coffee shop, Lake Gaston Coffee Company, and they sell almost as fast as I can make them.

INTRODUCTION

I love to cook and eat just about anything, but what I cook the most is what I grew up on, which is southern food. When most people think of southern food, the first thing that comes to mind are the staples like fried chicken, cornbread, biscuits and gravy, etc. While those are classics that southerners love, we also enjoy a wide variety of dishes from all over the world. Go to a pot luck dinner and you'll find not only the classic staples, but also Italian, Asian, Mexican, and Greek dishes. If there's one thing we love to do, it's eat!

The best thing about southern food is how diverse it is. No two recipes are the same. Some folks use lard to fry with rather than vegetable oil. Some like vinegar-based barbecue sauce rather than ketchup-based. The point is, even though recipes vary greatly, every recipe is made with heart and is delicious.

To me, southern food is comfort food. It's something that makes you feel warm inside. I wanted every recipe in the book to convey comfort whether it's a quick and easy meal or a dish that takes a little more time and effort. I also wanted the recipes in this book to be something that folks would cook on a regular basis, not something that requires hours of prep and hard to find ingredients. Southern food is prepared with heart and love, so that you can sit around with your family and friends and enjoy good food and great company. That's the very definition of comfort to me.

INTRODUCTION

INSPIRATION: "THE WRESTLER"

Throughout our lives everyone of us has had someone that has crossed our paths that has inspired us, motivated us, or to simply put it, given us a good kick in the rear. I have had many people in my life that have done all of those things, but the one person who inspired me the most to do a cookbook is someone whose name I don't even know.

My job, the one that I actually get paid for, is at a local emergency room doing CAT scans. I have worked the weekend night shift for the past eleven years and believe me when I say that I have seen it all! It takes a lot to surprise me.

One night, a few years ago, I received an order to do a scan of a patient's lower back. I looked at the order and the patient's history and saw I was doing the scan because the patient had been body slammed. I knew there was an interesting story there.

I entered the patient's room, introduced myself, and told him that I was taking him for some images of his lower back. The patient was a very polite young man in his early 20's. I would describe him as a small build or even scrawny. I asked him what happened that brought him into the ER and he said that he was a minor league wrestler and he was body slammed. Now, I don't like to label people, but he could obviously tell by my immediate facial expression that I was surprised. He immediately added "I know, I know...I don't look like a wrestler."

I didn't in any way want to be rude or offend this guy, but I had to ask him why he, someone of his stature and build, would ever want to do something like wrestle. He responded quite simply with, "Because it's what I love to do, it's my passion." He then added, "What's your passion, what is something that you've always wanted to do?"

Without even thinking I said, "I love to cook and my dream is to one day write my own cookbook." He responded by saying, "Well, why don't you?"

I was stumped! I thought to myself, if this tiny thing of a person can freakin' wrestle, why can't I make recipes and put them down in a book? I decided then and there that I would do just that...and here it is! No one but my family and close friends might ever look at this thing, but that's okay...the point is that I did it. I made my dream a reality and I owe that kick in the butt to the guy who I only know as "The Wrestler".

APPETIZERS

APPETIZERS

APPETIZERS

PIMENTO CHEESE

SERVES: 12-16

A favorite southern classic used as a dip or sandwich spread.

INGREDIENTS

- 24 oz sharp cheddar cheese, shredded
- 8 oz pepperjack cheese, shredded
- 4 oz cream cheese, room temperature
- 3/4 cup mayonnaise
- 1 jalapeño pepper, minced (seeded)
- 1 tablespoon sugar
- 1 teaspoon garlic powder
- 1/2 teaspoon onion powder
- 1/2 teaspoon salt
- 1/8 teaspoon black pepper
- 4 oz jar of pimentos
- 1 tablespoon fresh parsley, chopped

DIRECTIONS

- Mix all ingredients together in a large bowl until combined.
- Refrigerate in an air tight container.
- Serve with crackers or on toast.
- *Note: leave the jalapeño seeds in if you like it extra spicy!*

APPETIZERS

LADY FINGERS

MAKES: 36 cookies

These little cookies covered in confectioners' sugar are a delicious party favorite. Betcha can't eat just one!

INGREDIENTS

- 2 cups all-purpose flour
- 1 cup confectioners' sugar, divided
- 3/4 cup (1-1/2 sticks) unsalted butter, room temperature
- 1 teaspoon vanilla extract
- 1 teaspoon almond extract
- 1-1/2 tablespoons iced water
- 1/2 cup pecans, chopped

DIRECTIONS

- Preheat the oven to 350 degrees and line a half sheet pan with parchment paper.
- Add the flour, 1/2 cup confectioners' sugar, butter, vanilla extract, almond extract, and iced water to a medium sized bowl. Knead ingredients together with your hands until the dough comes together. Knead in the pecans.
- Take a tablespoon sized portion of the dough, roll into a log and place on the sheet pan. Repeat for the remaining dough.
- Bake for 15 minutes or until slightly browned.
- Add 1/2 cup confectioners' sugar to a bowl. While the lady fingers are still hot, dredge them in the confectioners' sugar until coated, shaking off any excess.

APPETIZERS

NACHO CHEESE DIP

SERVES: 16-20

A family party favorite! Anytime my family gets together and there's food involved, this is on the table.

INGREDIENTS

- 2 lbs ground beef
- 1 lb ground hot sausage
- 1 small onion, chopped
- 1 jalapeño pepper, diced (seeded)
- 10 oz jar of mild salsa
- 10.5 oz can cream of mushroom soup
- 1 package taco seasoning mix
- 24 oz (3 blocks) cream cheese

DIRECTIONS

- Brown the ground beef and sausage and drain.
- Mix all ingredients in a slow cooker on high for 1-1/2 hours until the cream cheese is melted. Turn the slow cooker to low to keep warm.
- Serve with tortilla chips.

GUACAMOLE

SERVES: 4-6

This Mexican specialty can be used as a dip or condiment.
The fresh ingredients are what really makes it stand out and is always a crowd pleaser.

INGREDIENTS

- 4 ripe avocados, sliced in half with pit removed
- 1/2 cup red onion, diced
- 2 roma tomatoes, diced
- 1 jalapeño pepper, minced (seeded)
- 1 garlic clove, minced
- 1 teaspoon salt
- 1/2 cup fresh cilantro, roughly chopped
- Juice from 2 limes

DIRECTIONS

- Scoop out the avocado halves with a spoon and add to a large bowl.
- Finley dice the avocados with a knife or a masher, depending how chunky you want it to be.
- Add the lime juice, onion, tomatoes, jalapeño pepper, garlic, salt, and cilantro and stir together.
- Serve immediately.

APPETIZERS

Fried green tomatoes are the quintessential southern summer appetizer and they're so easy to make. In a matter of minutes you'll be serving up these crispy mouthwatering favorites.

FRIED GREEN TOMATOES

SERVES: 4

INGREDIENTS

- 2 large green tomatoes, sliced 1/4 inch thick
- vegetable oil
- 1 cup all-purpose flour
- 1 tablespoon salt
- 1 tablespoon black pepper
- 2 eggs
- 1 cup Italian bread crumbs
- balsamic vinegar

DIRECTIONS

- Add the vegetable oil to a cast iron skillet to a depth of 1/2 inch. Heat over medium-high heat.
- In a medium sized bowl, stir together flour, salt, and pepper. In a second bowl, whisk together eggs and 1 tablespoon water. In a third bowl, add the bread crumbs.
- Dredge each slice of tomato in the flour mixture, then the egg mixture, and finally the bread crumbs.
- Once the oil reaches 350 degrees, according to a candy thermometer, fry the tomatoes in batches of 3-4 slices per batch while being careful not to overcrowd the pan.
- Cook for 2 minutes on each side until golden brown and drain on paper towels.
- Drizzle with balsamic vinegar and serve hot.

STEVEN BAKER | www.StevenDoesFood.com

APPETIZERS

BACON WRAPPED CHICKEN BITES

SERVES: 8-12

Great as an appetizer, finger food for parties, snacks, or even as a main dish.

INGREDIENTS

- 3 boneless, skinless chicken breasts cut into 1-inch cubes
- 1 lb bacon, cut into thirds
- black pepper
- 2 cups BBQ sauce

DIRECTIONS

- Preheat oven to 375 degrees and place a wire baking rack in a half sheet pan lined with aluminum foil.
- Wrap each chicken piece with a bacon strip and place the bacon wrapped chicken on the baking rack.
- Sprinkle with pepper and bake for 45 minutes, flipping each piece halfway through cooking.
- Add the chicken to a large bowl and toss with BBQ sauce.

ROASTED PECANS

SERVES: 10-12

What's not to love about these classic holiday treats? The nutty earthy flavor of the pecans with the sweet cinnamon and sugar compliment each other perfectly.

INGREDIENTS

- 2-1/2 cups pecans, halved
- 4 tablespoons unsalted butter, melted
- 1/2 cup sugar
- 1-1/2 teaspoons cinnamon
- 1/4 teaspoon salt

DIRECTIONS

- Preheat the oven to 300 degrees and line a half sheet pan with parchment paper.
- In a large bowl, stir melted butter and pecans. Add sugar, cinnamon, and salt and stir until all the pecans are coated.
- Evenly spread the pecans onto the pan.
- Cook for 10 minutes, stir, then cook for another 10 minutes.
- Remove from the oven and allow to cool slightly.

APPETIZERS

SWEET POTATO RICE LETTUCE WRAPS

SERVES: 4-6

I'm always looking for ways to eat more healthy. I went to a cooking party once and the host had taken sweet potatoes, spiralized them, chopped them into "rice", and used them in a dish. They were fantastic! These wraps make for a wonderful healthy snack, lunch, or starter.

INGREDIENTS

- 2 sweet potatoes, peeled, spiralized, and roughly chopped
- olive oil
- 15 oz can whole kernel corn, drained
- 1 tablespoon garlic powder
- 2 tablespoons sriracha sauce
- 1/4 cup red onion, diced
- 1 bell pepper, diced
- 1 roma tomato, diced
- 1 head of bibb or butterhead lettuce
- fresh cilantro, roughly chopped
- fresh squeezed lime juice

DIRECTIONS

- Heat 2 tablespoons of olive oil in a large sauté pan or wok over medium-high heat.
- Add sweet potatoes, corn, and garlic powder and cook for 5 minutes or until potatoes are tender.
- Stir in the sriracha sauce, remove from heat, and set aside to cool.
- Once the sweet potato mixture has cooled, fold in the onions, bell pepper, and tomatoes.
- Spoon mixture into each lettuce leaf and top with cilantro and lime juice.

STEVEN BAKER | www.StevenDoesFood.com

APPETIZERS

COCONUT SHRIMP WITH SPICY AIOLI

SERVES: 4

These golden sweet shrimp are perfect for appetizers or even as the meal themselves. The golden coconut encrusted shrimp with the zesty tangy aioli gives the perfect balance of sweet and spicy.

INGREDIENTS

- 1 lb medium or large shrimp, cleaned with tails on
- 5 cups vegetable oil
- 2 cups shredded coconut
- 2 cups panko bread crumbs
- 1/2 tablespoon paprika
- 1 tablespoon garlic powder
- 1 teaspoon salt
- 1 teaspoon black pepper
- 2 eggs

DIRECTIONS

- In a medium pot, heat the vegetable oil over medium-high heat until the temperature reads 325 degrees on a candy thermometer.
- In a small bowl, beat the eggs with 1 tablespoon of water. In a large bowl, combine the coconut, panko bread crumbs, paprika, garlic powder, salt, and pepper. Coat each shrimp with the egg mixture then dredge the shrimp in the coconut mixture.
- Cook the shrimp in batches for 2-3 minutes until lightly browned and place the shrimp on a plate lined with paper towels. *See the next page for my Spicy Aioli recipe.*

SPICY AIOLI

INGREDIENTS

- 1 cup mayonnaise
- 1 jalapeno pepper, roughly chopped with seeds
- 1 teaspoon paprika
- ½ teaspoon cayenne pepper
- 2 garlic cloves
- ½ teaspoon salt
- ½ teaspoon black pepper
- Zest and juice from 1 lime

DIRECTIONS

- Add all ingredients to the bowl of a food processor and process until combined.

PENNIES FROM HEAVEN

SERVES: 16-20

These spicy little crackers are the perfect finger food for any party or just to have as a snack anytime you want. They go great along side cocktails and also with soups and salads.

INGREDIENTS

- 16 oz sharp cheddar cheese, shredded
- 1 cup (2 sticks) unsalted butter, room temperature
- 2-1/2 cups all-purpose flour, sifted
- 1-1/2 teaspoons cayenne pepper
- 1 teaspoon salt

DIRECTIONS

- Preheat the oven to 350 degrees and line 2 half sheet pans with parchment paper.
- In the bowl of a stand mixer fitted with the paddle attachment, mix together the cheese and butter until well combined.
- With the mixer on low, slowly add the flour a little at a time, stopping every so often to scrape down the sides of the bowl.
- Add the cayenne pepper and salt and mix to combine.
- Take about a teaspoon sized portion of the dough and roll into a ball. Place the ball on the sheet pan and flatten with your fingers. Repeat until both half sheet pans are full.
- Bake for 30 minutes until browned.

APPETIZERS

APPETIZERS

PIZZA POCKETS

SERVES: 24

My mom would make these when I was a kid for school parties or bake sales and they were always a hit. Recently, I was going through my grandmother's recipes and came across this one. Beside it she wrote "teenagers love these!" My grandmama knew what was cool!

INGREDIENTS

Dough:
- 2-1/2 cups all-purpose flour
- 1 teaspoon sugar
- 1 tablespoon baking powder
- 1/2 teaspoon baking soda
- 1/2 teaspoon salt
- 1/2 cup (1 stick) cold unsalted butter, cubed
- 1 cup buttermilk
- 1/2 cup cheddar cheese, shredded

Filling:
- 1 lb ground beef
- 1 lb mild sausage
- 14 oz jar pizza sauce
- 1-1/2 cups mozzarella cheese, shredded

DIRECTIONS

- In a large bowl, sift together flour, sugar, baking powder, baking soda, and salt. Place the bowl in the freezer for 10 minutes.
- Preheat the oven to 350 degrees and grease 2 muffin pans.
- In a large frying pan or skillet, brown the ground beef and sausage. Drain meat, wipe the pan clean, and add the meat back to the pan. Over low heat, stir in pizza sauce until warm. Stir in mozzarella cheese until melted and set aside.
- Add flour mixture and butter to the bowl of a food processor. Pulse several times until butter is the size of peas. Transfer flour and butter mixture back to the large bowl and gradually stir in the buttermilk. Stir in the cheddar cheese until combined. Continue to stir until the dough is formed.
- Dump the dough out onto a floured surface and knead until the dough becomes smooth. With a rolling pin, roll the dough out to about 1/8 inch thick. Using a biscuit cutter, cut out a round circle of dough and place in the muffin pan. Continue until the muffin pan is full.
- Spoon the pizza filling into the dough.
- Bake for 25-30 minutes until the dough is golden brown.

SOUPS & SALADS

SOUPS & SALADS

SOUPS & SALADS

HAMBURGER SOUP

SERVES: 6-8

This hearty soup that's loaded with flavorful ground beef and tender vegetables is perfect on a cold winter day. It's easy to throw together, and best of all, it's budget friendly.

INGREDIENTS

- 2lbs ground beef, browned and drained
- olive oil
- 1 large onion, chopped
- 2 whole carrots, diced
- 2 celery stalks, diced
- 1 tablespoon fresh thyme, chopped
- 2 garlic cloves, minced
- 8 cups beef stock
- 2 cups Yukon Gold potatoes, cut into cubes
- 1/2 cup green beans, ends trimmed and cut into pieces
- 2 bay leaves
- 1/2 teaspoon basil
- 1 teaspoon chili powder
- 2 teaspoons salt
- 1 teaspoon black pepper
- 1 cup frozen sweet corn

DIRECTIONS

- In a large pot or Dutch oven, add 1 tablespoon of olive oil over medium heat.
- Once the oil is hot, add the onions, carrots, celery, and thyme and cook for 5 minutes until tender. Add the garlic and cook for 1 minute.
- Add the beef stock, cooked ground beef, green beans, potatoes, bay leaves, basil, chili powder, salt, and pepper. Bring to a boil then reduce the heat to low. Cover and simmer for 20 minutes. Add the corn and simmer for 10 minutes.
- Remove the bay leaves and taste to see if more salt is needed.
- Serve hot.

SOUPS & SALADS

POTATO & SAUSAGE SOUP

SERVES: 6-8

This rich and creamy soup is the perfect meal for those cold weeknights after being at work all day. It's a snap to make and absolutely scrumptious.

INGREDIENTS

- 1 lb ground sausage
- 6 tablespoons unsalted butter, divided
- 1 large onion, diced
- 1 whole carrot, diced
- 2 teaspoons fresh thyme, chopped
- 3 garlic cloves, minced
- 4 cups chicken stock
- 3-4 russet or Yukon Gold potatoes, diced
- salt and black pepper
- 3 tablespoons all-purpose flour
- 2 cups whole milk
- 1/2 cup heavy cream

DIRECTIONS

- In a large stock pot or Dutch oven, brown the sausage, drain, and set aside.
- Add 2 tablespoons of butter to the pot over medium heat. Once the butter is melted, add onions, carrots, and thyme and cook for 5 minutes until onions are soft and translucent. Add the garlic and cook for 1 minute.
- Pour the chicken stock in and scrape the browned bits from the bottom of the pot.
- Add the potatoes, sausage, 1 teaspoon salt, and 1/2 teaspoon black pepper. Bring to a boil, then reduce heat to low, and cover and simmer for 30 minutes.
- In a medium sized sauce pan, add the remaining 4 tablespoons of butter over medium heat. Once melted, add the flour and vigorously whisk together for 1 minute. Slowly stir in the milk and heavy cream. Stir in the mixture to the soup. Taste to see if more salt and pepper is needed.
- Serve hot.

SOUPS & SALADS

STEVEN BAKER | www.StevenDoesFood.com

SOUPS & SALADS

SOUPS & SALADS

TURKEY CHILI

SERVES: 6-8

This chili is not only tasty, but it's healthy as well. The perfect blend of protein and spices simmered for several hours makes this a go-to hearty meal.

INGREDIENTS

- 3 lbs ground turkey
- olive oil
- 1 medium onion, diced
- 4-5 garlic cloves, minced
- 1 yellow bell pepper, diced
- 1 jalapeño pepper, diced (seeded)
- 15 oz can tomato sauce
- 12 oz can tomato paste
- 28 oz can diced tomatoes
- (2) 16 oz cans kidney beans, drained
- 1 tablespoon chili powder
- 1 teaspoon coriander
- 1 teaspoon cumin
- 1 teaspoon garlic powder
- 1 teaspoon onion powder
- 1 teaspoon paprika
- 1 teaspoon salt
- 1 teaspoon black pepper
- 1/4 teaspoon red pepper flakes
- 3 cups beef stock
- green onions, chopped
- sour cream
- cheddar cheese, shredded

DIRECTIONS

- In a large pan or skillet, brown the ground turkey, drain, and set aside.
- In a large pot or Dutch oven, heat 1 tablespoon of olive oil over medium-high heat. Once the oil is hot, add onions and cook until soft and translucent, about 5 minutes. Add garlic and cook for 1 minute.
- Add the bell pepper, jalapeño pepper, tomato sauce, tomato paste, diced tomatoes, kidney beans, spices, ground turkey, and beef stock and bring to a boil. Turn the heat to low and simmer covered for 2 hours, stirring occasionally.
- Serve hot topped with green onions, sour cream, and cheese.

SOUPS & SALADS

BROCCOLI ALMOND SALAD

SERVES: 6-8

A simple and quick salad made with fresh ingredients. Makes for a wonderful appetizer or side dish.

INGREDIENTS

- 8 cups broccoli florets (about 4 heads of fresh broccoli)
- 1/2 cup celery, diced
- 1/4 cup red onion, diced
- 1/4 cup cooked bacon, chopped
- 3/4 cup mayonnaise
- 2 tablespoons honey
- juice from 1 lemon
- 1 tablespoon fresh dill, chopped
- 1/2 teaspoon black pepper
- 1/2 cup sliced almonds
- green onions, chopped

DIRECTIONS

- In a large bowl, combine the broccoli florets, celery, onion, and bacon.
- In a small bowl, whisk together the mayonnaise, honey, lemon juice, dill, and black pepper. Pour over the broccoli mixture and toss to coat. Stir in the almonds.
- Serve and top with green onions.

SOUPS & SALADS

CHICKEN & RICE SOUP

SERVES: 6-8

There are two things that make you feel better when you're feeling under the weather: daytime TV and a good bowl of chicken and rice soup. I roast the chicken instead of boiling it to maximize the flavor.

INGREDIENTS

- 3 boneless skinless chicken breasts
- olive oil
- salt and black pepper
- 1 small onion, diced
- 2 whole carrots, diced
- 2 celery stalks, diced
- 4 garlic cloves, minced
- 1 tablespoon fresh thyme, chopped
- 8 cups chicken stock
- 4 cups water
- 1-1/2 cups white rice
- parsley, chopped

DIRECTIONS

- Preheat the oven to 425 degrees.
- Drizzle the chicken breasts with olive oil and sprinkle with salt and pepper to taste.
- Add chicken breasts to a sheet pan and bake for 45 minutes then set aside to cool. Cut the chicken into bite sized pieces.
- In a large pot, add 2 tablespoons of olive oil over medium heat. Add the onions, carrots, celery, and thyme and cook until the vegetables are tender, about 5 minutes.
- Add garlic and cook for 1 minute. Add chicken stock, water, rice, 1-1/2 tsp salt, and 1 tsp black pepper. Bring to a boil.
- Reduce the heat to low, cover, and simmer for 20 minutes.
- Stir in chicken pieces, cover, and cook for 10 more minutes.
- Serve hot topped with parsley.

STEVEN BAKER | www.StevenDoesFood.com

SOUPS & SALADS

CHICKPEA JAR SALAD

MAKES: 32 oz jar

I'm always trying to find quick and easy ways to eat on the go without skimping on flavor and jar salads are perfect for that. There are countless ways to make a jar salad. For this particular one, I use chickpeas for protein added with colorful veggies. Chickpeas have a great earthy taste and texture that I love. I prepare several of these at a time and lunch is covered for the week.

INGREDIENTS

- 1/4 cup salad dressing
- 1/3 cup chickpeas, drained and washed
- 1/4 cup cherry tomatoes, sliced
- 1/4 cup cucumber, peeled and cubed
- 2-3 tablespoons red onions, chopped
- 1 cup mixed baby greens
- 1/4 cup cheddar cheese, shredded
- 2-3 tablespoons sliced almonds

DIRECTIONS

- In a 32 oz Mason jar, layer the salad by:
  1) dressing **2)** chickpeas **3)** tomatoes, cucumbers, onions **4)** mixed greens **5)** cheese, almonds
- Put the lid on the jar and store in the refrigerator.
- When ready to eat, shake the jar to mix all the ingredients and dump into a bowl or plate.

WATERGATE SALAD

SERVES: 6-8

This classic, that goes by several names, is a simple dish that can be served as a side or dessert.

INGREDIENTS

- 3.4 oz pack instant pistachio pudding
- 20 oz can crushed pineapple, with juice
- 1 cup miniature marshmallows
- 16 oz tub whipped topping
- 1 cup pecans, roughly chopped
- maraschino cherries

DIRECTIONS

- Mix all ingredients except for the maraschino cherries together and chill for 2 hours.
- Serve and top each portion with maraschino cherries.

SOUPS & SALADS

CHICKEN & VEGETABLE SOUP

SERVES: 6-8

This is a timeless recipe that I make all the time. If my grandmother's kitchen had a distinct smell, this soup would be it. Every time I make it I'm filled with so many memories of her. This soup goes great with fried chicken!

INGREDIENTS

- 1 whole chicken, cut into 9 pieces
- several sprigs of rosemary, thyme, and dill
- salt and black pepper
- 4 cups chicken stock
- 2 whole carrots, diced
- 2 celery stalks, diced
- 1 medium onion, diced
- 4 garlic cloves, minced
- 28 oz can diced tomatoes
- 2 cups frozen butter beans
- 2 cups russet potatoes (about 2 potatoes), cut into small cubes
- 2 cups frozen sweet corn
- 15 oz can cream style corn

DIRECTIONS

- Place the chicken in a large stock pot and fill with water.
- Take the sprigs of rosemary, thyme, and dill and tie together with kitchen twine and add to the pot.
- Add 1 tablespoon salt and 1/2 tablespoon black pepper. Bring to a boil and cook for 45 minutes.
- Remove the chicken and set aside to cool. Set the pot aside, preserving the stock.
- Once the chicken is cooled, debone and add the meat back to the pot.
- Add the 4 cups of extra chicken stock, carrots, celery, onion, garlic, diced tomatoes, and butter beans. Taste and add more salt and pepper as needed.
- Bring to a boil and cook for 30 minutes, stirring occasionally.
- Add potatoes and cook for 30 minutes, stirring occasionally.
- Add frozen corn and cream style corn then reduce the heat to low. Simmer for 15 minutes then remove the rosemary, thyme, and dill.
- Serve hot.

STEVEN BAKER | www.StevenDoesFood.com

BUTTERNUT SQUASH SOUP

SERVES: 6-8

This warm and cozy soup has quickly become a favorite meal when fall comes around. It's bursting with a variety of flavors that all marry together to make a satisfying and robust soup. Instead of using an immersion blender, you can also smooth out the soup in a food processor or blender.

INGREDIENTS

- 4 cups onions, roughly chopped (4-5 medium sized onions)
- 2 teaspoons fresh thyme, minced
- olive oil
- 4-1/2 to 5 cups butternut squash, peeled and roughly diced (2 butternut squash)
- 1 cup apple cider beer
- 1 tablespoon salt
- 1/2 tablespoon black pepper
- 1 tablespoon curry powder
- 1 teaspoon turmeric
- 1/4 teaspoon cumin
- 2 sage leaves
- 2 sprigs of rosemary
- 3 cups chicken stock, divided
- 1/4 cup heavy cream
- cooked bacon, roughly chopped

DIRECTIONS

- In a large stockpot or Dutch oven, add 2 tablespoons of olive oil over medium heat.
- Once the oil is hot, add the onions and thyme and cook until the onions are soft and translucent, about 5 minutes. Add the beer and cook until reduced, about 5 minutes.
- Add the butternut squash, spices and herbs, and 2 cups of chicken stock and bring to a boil. Turn the heat down to low, cover and simmer for 45 minutes.
- Remove the lid, add 1 cup of chicken stock, and process the soup using an immersion blender until smooth. Taste and add more salt if needed. Stir in heavy cream.
- Serve hot topped with bacon.

SOUPS & SALADS

BREADS

BREADS

SWEET POTATO BISCUITS

MAKES: 18 biscuits

I had never heard of sweet potato biscuits until a few years ago, but once I tried them I was hooked. They're soft, flaky, and sweet. They MUST be served hot out of the oven and drizzled with honey... heaven!

INGREDIENTS

- 1 sweet potato, peeled and cubed
- 1-1/2 cups cake flour
- 1/2 cup all-purpose flour
- 2 tablespoons baking powder
- 1/2 teaspoon baking soda
- 1/2 teaspoon salt
- 2 tablespoons sugar
- 1/2 cup (1 stick) cold unsalted butter, cut into small cubes
- honey (optional)

DIRECTIONS

- Preheat the oven to 425 degrees and line a sheet pan with parchment paper.
- In a medium sized sauce pan, bring about 5 cups of water to a boil. Add the sweet potato cubes and cook until fork tender, about 10-15 minutes. Drain, mash, and set aside to cool completely.
- In a food processor, add the cake flour, all-purpose flour, baking powder, baking soda, salt, and sugar. Pulse several times to combine. Add the butter and pulse several times until butter is the size of peas. Add the mashed sweet potato and process until the dough forms.
- Dump the dough onto a floured board and knead to form a disc. Wrap in plastic wrap and refrigerate for 30 minutes.
- On a floured board, roll the dough out to 1/4 inch thick and cut out biscuits using a biscuit cutter. Place the biscuits on the sheet pan and bake for 10-15 minutes until golden brown.
- Drizzle honey over hot biscuits.

SKILLET CORNBREAD

MAKES: 10" round

This cornbread has so much richness and sweetness that it could be served as dessert. It's soft fluffy center and slightly crisp edges make the perfect compliment to any meal.

INGREDIENTS

- 1-3/4 cup yellow cornmeal
- 1/4 cup all-purpose flour
- 1 tablespoon baking powder
- 1 teaspoon baking soda
- 1 teaspoon salt
- 1/2 cup sugar
- 2 eggs
- 1 cup buttermilk
- 1/2 cup (1 stick) unsalted butter, divided
- 2 tablespoons vegetable shortening

DIRECTIONS

- Place a 10-inch cast iron skillet into the oven and preheat to 425 degrees.
- In a medium sized bowl, whisk together the cornmeal, flour, baking powder, baking soda, salt, and sugar and set aside.
- In a small bowl, whisk the eggs and buttermilk together. Fold the egg mixture in with the cornmeal mixture until well combined.
- In a small sauce pan over medium heat, melt the vegetable shortening and 6 tablespoons of butter. Mix the melted shortening and butter in with the cornbread batter reserving 1 tablespoon of the butter mixture.
- Remove the cast iron skillet from the oven and add the 1 tablespoon of the reserved melted butter. Add the cornbread batter to the skillet and place back in the oven.
- Bake for 15 minutes until the cornbread is golden brown and remove from the oven.
- Top with remaining 2 tablespoons of butter.

BREADS

BREADS

BUTTERMILK BISCUITS

MAKES: 8-10 biscuits

These biscuits are soft, flaky, and buttery. Is there a better combination? The secret is to use very cold ingredients so the dough will rise and produce amazing biscuits.

INGREDIENTS

- 2-1/2 cups all-purpose flour plus more for kneading
- 1 teaspoon sugar
- 1 tablespoon baking powder
- 1/2 teaspoon baking soda
- 1/2 teaspoon salt
- 1/2 cup (1 stick) cold unsalted butter, cubed
- 1 cup buttermilk

DIRECTIONS

- Preheat the oven to 425 degrees. Line a sheet pan with parchment paper.
- Sift together the flour, sugar, baking powder, baking soda, and salt in a large bowl. Place the bowl in the freezer for 10 minutes.
- Add the flour mixture and butter to the bowl of a food processor. Pulse several times until the butter is the size of peas.
- Transfer the flour mixture back to the large bowl and gradually stir in the buttermilk. Continue to stir until the dough is formed.
- Dump the dough onto a floured surface and knead until the dough becomes smooth. With a rolling pin, roll the dough out to about 1/2 to 1/4 inches thick. Cut out the biscuits with a biscuit cutter and place on the sheet pan.
- Bake for 15-18 minutes until the biscuits turn golden brown.

GRANDDADDY'S SOUTHERN BISCUITS

MAKES: 6-9 biscuits

My grandfather would make these biscuits with just about every meal he made. They have more of a crunch to them than buttermilk biscuits have, which is what I love about them. My favorite way to eat them is smothered in gravy!

INGREDIENTS

- 2-3/4 cups self-rising flour, divided
- 1 tablespoon vegetable shortening
- 1 cup buttermilk

DIRECTIONS

- Preheat the oven to 425 degrees and line a sheet pan with parchment paper.
- Sift 2 cups of the flour over a medium sized bowl. Add the vegetable shortening and buttermilk. Knead together with a fork until the shortening and buttermilk are incorporated, being careful not to over mix.
- Add 3/4 cups flour to a board. Drop about 3 tablespoons of the biscuit dough into the flour and roll into a ball. Shake off any excess flour, place on the sheet pan, and slightly flatten with your hand. Repeat until all of the dough is used.
- Bake for 30 minutes until browned.

BREADS

BREADS

RUSTIC DUTCH OVEN BREAD

MAKES: 8" loaf

This fancy loaf of bread is not only delicious with its crunchy crust and soft moist interior, but it's also surprisingly easy to make. One surefire way to impress guests is to pull a fresh warm loaf of bread right out of the oven.

INGREDIENTS

- 1 package (2-1/4 teaspoons) active dry yeast
- 1-1/2 teaspoons salt
- 1-1/2 cups warm water
- 3 cups bread flour

DIRECTIONS

- In a large bowl, whisk together the yeast, salt, and warm water and set aside for 5 minutes for the yeast to dissolve.
- Add in the flour and stir until the dough comes together (the dough will be sticky). Cover with plastic wrap and set in a warm place for 2-3 hours until the dough doubles in size.
- Put the Dutch oven with the lid on in a cold oven and then preheat the oven to 450 degrees. Allow the Dutch oven to sit in the oven for 15 minutes after it's preheated to get very hot.
- Transfer the dough to a floured surface. With your hands or a pastry scraper, fold the dough in on itself several times. Transfer the dough to the center of a sheet of parchment paper, about 9"x13", and cover with a towel for 30 minutes. You can shape the dough however you like and can also score the top with a knife.
- Place the dough with the parchment paper underneath in the hot Dutch oven and cover with the lid. Put the Dutch oven back into the oven and bake for 30 minutes. Remove the lid and bake for 10-15 minutes until the bread is golden brown.
- Take the bread out of the Dutch oven by the parchment paper.

HOECAKES

MAKES: 10-12 cakes

Hoecakes, also called fried cornbread, are a staple here in the south. They go great with any meal. Cook in batches so the temperature of the oil stays hot to ensure they come out crunchy.

INGREDIENTS

- 3 cups yellow cornmeal
- 1-1/2 teaspoons salt
- 1 teaspoon black pepper
- 2-1/4 cups water
- vegetable oil

DIRECTIONS

- Fill half of a large frying pan or cast-iron skillet with vegetable oil and heat over medium-high until the temperature of the oil reaches 360-380 degrees.
- In a large bowl, mix the cornmeal, salt, pepper, and water until combined. Working in batches of 3 or 4 pieces at a time, drop 1/4 cup of batter per piece into the hot oil.
- Cook until the hoecake turns brown and crisp then flip and brown the other side.
- Serve warm.

BREADS

*Everyone's favorite part of any meal is the bread. Change my mind!
These rolls are soft and buttery and can easily steal the main course's thunder.*

DINNER ROLLS

MAKES: 12-13 rolls

INGREDIENTS

- 1 cup whole milk
- 1 (2-1/4 teaspoons) package active dry yeast
- 1 cup (2 sticks) unsalted butter, room temp
- 2 eggs
- 3-1/2 cups bread flour
- 3 tablespoons sugar
- 1 teaspoon salt

DIRECTIONS

- In a small sauce pan, heat the milk until warmed, about 80-90 degrees.
- In the bowl of a stand mixer fitted with the dough hook attachment, add the milk and yeast and let stand for 5 minutes.
- Add the butter, eggs, flour, sugar, and salt and knead on medium speed until the ball of dough forms.
- Transfer the dough to a large greased bowl, cover, and let the dough rise in a warm place for 2 hours.
- Punch down the center of the dough to release any air. Divide the dough into equal pieces and place on a sheet pan lined with parchment paper or in a cast iron skillet. Cover and let sit for 1 hour.
- Preheat the oven to 350 degrees. Uncover the rolls and bake for 15-20 minutes until lightly browned.
- Serve warm with butter.

STEVEN BAKER | www.StevenDoesFood.com

BREADS

BREADS

BLUEBERRY MUFFINS

MAKES: 12 muffins

Blueberry muffins are my favorite go-to breakfast food. They're great anytime but best hot right out of the oven. You can also use other berries like raspberries, blackberries, or if you like to live life on the wild side, a mixture of all three!

INGREDIENTS

- 2 cups fresh blueberries
- 1 cup plus 2 tablespoons sugar, divided
- 3 cups all-purpose flour
- 1 tablespoon baking powder
- 1/2 teaspoon baking soda
- 1 tablespoon cinnamon
- 1/2 teaspoon salt
- 1 cup (2 sticks) unsalted butter, room temperature
- 1 cup whole milk
- 1 teaspoon lemon zest
- 1 teaspoon vanilla extract
- 2 eggs
- turbinado cane sugar

DIRECTIONS

- Preheat the oven to 375 degrees. Line a muffin tin with paper liners.
- In a medium sauce pan, cook the blueberries and 2 tablespoons of sugar over medium-high heat for 4-5 minutes until the sauce forms, stirring constantly. Remove from heat and set aside to cool.
- Over a large bowl, sift the flour, baking powder, baking soda, cinnamon, and salt and set aside.
- In the bowl of a stand mixer fitted with the paddle attachment, beat the butter and 1 cup sugar until creamy. With the mixer on low, slowly add the flour mixture and the milk a little at a time starting and ending with the flour mixture. Add the lemon zest, vanilla extract, and eggs and mix until combined. Fold the cooled blueberry sauce into the batter.
- Using an ice cream scoop, scoop the batter into the muffin liners. Sprinkle the top of each muffin with the turbinado cane sugar.
- Bake for 15-20 minutes until the muffins are golden brown.

SUPPERS

SUPPERS

HAMBURGERS & GRAVY

SERVES: 4

This dish is the very definition of comfort food. These juicy hamburgers smothered in lip smacking gravy is to die for. It's a requirement that these be served along side mashed potatoes and biscuits!

INGREDIENTS

- 2 lbs ground beef
- kosher salt
- black pepper
- 1/2 tablespoon garlic powder
- 1/2 tablespoon onion powder
- 1/4 teaspoon ground ginger
- 1 tablespoon fresh thyme, chopped
- 1 large yellow onion, sliced
- 1-1/2 cup portobello mushrooms, sliced
- 1/4 cup all-purpose flour
- 4 cups beef stock

DIRECTIONS

- In a large bowl, add the ground beef, 1 tablespoon salt, 1/2 tablespoon pepper, garlic powder, onion powder, ginger, and thyme and mix together with a fork. Shape out 8-10 patties.
- Heat a large pan or skillet over medium-high heat. Once hot, add the hamburger patties, onions, and mushrooms. Cook for 5-6 minutes on each side.
- Remove hamburgers, onions, and mushrooms and set aside. Remove grease from the skillet, reserving 1/4 cup for the gravy.
- To make the gravy, add the 1/4 cup of grease back to the pan. Once hot, add the flour with a pinch of salt and pepper and whisk vigorously until the flour turns dark brown. Whisk in the beef stock. Taste the gravy to see if any more salt is needed.
- Add the hamburgers, onions, and mushrooms back to the pan and simmer uncovered for 20 minutes.

SUPPERS

FRIED CHICKEN

SERVES: 4

You can't get more southern than fried chicken! This chicken is bursting with flavor, from the marinade to the breading and even the oil that it fries in. Deep fried to golden perfection then finished off in the oven for a crispy and juicy southern classic.

SUPPERS

INGREDIENTS

- whole chicken cut into 8 pieces
- 2 tablespoons paprika
- 2 tablespoon black pepper
- 1 tablespoon garlic powder
- 1 teaspoon onion powder
- 1 teaspoon dried thyme
- 1/4 teaspoon cayenne pepper
- kosher salt
- 1 cup buttermilk
- 1 egg
- hot sauce, such as Texas Pete
- 1-1/2 cups all-purpose flour
- 1/2 cup corn starch
- 1 teaspoon baking powder
- 8-9 cups peanut oil
- several sprigs of fresh rosemary and thyme
- 1 whole head garlic with each clove smashed

DIRECTIONS

- In a small bowl, mix together the paprika, black pepper, garlic powder, onion powder, thyme, cayenne pepper, and 1 tablespoon salt. Set aside.
- In a medium bowl, whisk together the buttermilk, egg, several dashes of hot sauce, and 1 tablespoon of the spice mix. Pour the mixture into a large zipper-lock bag and add the chicken pieces. Flip the bag over several times to coat the chicken. Refrigerate for 4 hours.
- Preheat the oven to 350 degrees. Add a baking rack in a half sheet pan.
- In a large pot or Dutch oven, add the peanut oil, rosemary and thyme, and smashed garlic. Using a candy or instant read thermometer, heat the oil until approximately 360 degrees.
- In a large bowl, stir together the flour, corn starch, baking powder, pinch of salt, the rest of the spice mixture, and 3 tablespoons of the buttermilk marinade. Dredge each chicken piece in the flour mixture, coating each piece. Shake off any excess flour and set chicken aside.
- When the oil is ready, remove the rosemary, thyme, and garlic from the oil with a strainer. Add the chicken pieces to the oil in batches, being careful not to over crowd the pot. Cook the chicken until golden brown, about 5 minutes.
- Remove from the oil and place on the wire rack. Repeat with the remaining chicken pieces. Place the sheet pan in the oven and cook for 20-25 minutes until the breast reads 150 degrees and the leg reads 165 degrees on an instant read thermometer.
- Sprinkle with salt and serve hot.

SUPPERS

SUNDAY NIGHT POT ROAST

SERVES: 4

Whenever I would hear the words "pot roast", it always made me think of dry, tasteless shoe leather. This dish couldn't be farther from that. The meat is seared to lock in all the juicy flavor then cooked slowly for a few hours making the entire dish flavorful and succulent. This is perfect to make on a lazy afternoon and then eat the leftover for lunch the next day.

INGREDIENTS

- 1 chuck roast, 3-4 lbs
- salt and black pepper
- olive oil
- 5 whole carrots, chopped
- 1 large onion, chopped
- 3 celery stalks, chopped
- 4 garlic cloves, minced
- 1 cup red wine, such as merlot
- 4 cups beef stock
- 28 oz can crushed tomatoes
- 1 tablespoon Worcestershire sauce
- 1 bunch of fresh rosemary and thyme, tied together with kitchen twine
- Cooked white or basmati rice

DIRECTIONS

- Preheat the oven to 300 degrees.
- Pat the chuck roast dry with a paper towel and generously add salt and pepper to both sides.
- In a Dutch oven, add 3 tablespoons of olive oil over high heat. Once the oil is hot, add the chuck roast and sear for 2-3 minutes each side. Remove the roast and set aside.
- Turn the heat down to medium and add 1-2 tablespoons more olive oil. Add the carrots, onions, and celery and cook for 5 minutes until tender. Add the garlic and cook for 1 minute.
- Add the wine and scrape the browned bits from the bottom of the pot. Cook until the wine is reduced by half, about 3-4 minutes. Add the beef stock, crush tomatoes, Worcestershire sauce, bunch of rosemary and thyme, 1 teaspoon salt, and 1/2 teaspoon pepper. Bring to a boil then cover the pot with the lid and place in the oven. Cook for 2 1/2 hours.
- When done, discard the rosemary and thyme bunch. Serve hot over rice.

SUPPERS

SUPPERS

CHEESY SHELLS WITH MEAT SAUCE

SERVES: 8

This was the first meal I ever cooked for my husband and he still asks for it all the time. The pasta shells are stuffed with tons of cheese, then topped with homemade meat sauce and, finally, more cheese.

INGREDIENTS

- 1lb ground beef or turkey
- 1lb ground sausage
- 1 medium onion
- olive oil
- 3 garlic cloves, minced
- 1 bell pepper, diced
- 1 cup portobello mushrooms, diced
- 1 28oz can diced tomatoes
- 1 8oz can tomato sauce
- 1 6oz can tomato paste
- 1 tablespoon Italian seasoning
- 1 teaspoon chili powder
- 1 teaspoon oregano
- 1 teaspoon salt
- 1 teaspoon black pepper
- 1/2 teaspoon basil
- 1/2 teaspoon sugar
- 1/4 teaspoon red pepper flakes
- 2 bay leaves
- 1/4 cup ketchup
- 1/3 cup chicken stock
- 1 box jumbo shells
- 2 cups mozzarella cheese, shredded
- 2 cups sharp cheddar cheese, shredded
- freshly grated parmesan cheese
- parsley, roughly chopped

DIRECTIONS

- Brown the ground beef and sausage, drain, and set aside.
- In a large pot, heat 1 tablespoon of olive oil over medium heat. When the oil is hot, add the onions and cook until soft and translucent, about 5 minutes. Add the garlic and cook for 1 minute.
- Add the bell pepper, mushrooms, diced tomatoes, tomato sauce, tomato paste, spices, ketchup, and chicken stock and bring to a boil. Reduce the heat to low, cover, and simmer for 1 hour.
- Preheat the oven to 350 degrees.
- Cook the jumbo shells according to the box's directions. Drain the shells and let cool.
- Stuff each shell with the mozzarella and cheddar cheese and place in a 9"x13" baking dish. Spoon the meat sauce over the shells and top with remaining mozzarella and cheddar cheese. Cover the dish with aluminum foil and bake for 30 minutes.
- Remove the foil and bake for 15 minutes until the cheese is melted and bubbly.
- Serve topped with parmesan cheese and parsley.

CHICKENS ON THE GRILL

SERVES: 4

Every time my family gets together we have my dad's chickens on the grill. Rain or shine, blizzard or hurricane, there's no question that these will be on the menu. They cook slowly on the grill, resulting in moist flavorful meat and crisp skin. Use the leftover vinegar sauce for dipping!

INGREDIENTS

- 1 whole chicken, 3-4lbs
- 6 cups apple cider vinegar
- 1/2 cup (1 stick) unsalted butter
- 1 tablespoon red pepper flakes
- table salt

DIRECTIONS

- Set the grill for indirect heat: for charcoal, ready the coals and position them in 2 piles leaving a clear space in between the 2 piles. For gas with 3+ burners, light the first and third burners leaving the middle off. Set for medium heat.
- Cut the wings off the chicken and set aside. Butterfly the chicken by cutting through the breast bone, open the chicken up, and then flatten with the palm of your hand. Generously salt both sides of the chicken and both wings.
- In a medium sauce pan, add vinegar, butter, and red pepper flakes over high heat. Bring to a boil then remove from heat.
- When the grill is ready, place the chicken and wings skin side up directly over the cleared area of the grill. Cook for 15-20 minutes basting with the vinegar sauce several times.
- Flip the chicken, add more salt, and cook for 15 minutes basting several times. Flip again and salt. Cook for 15 minutes basting several times. Flip once more and cook for 15 minutes basting several times.
- Move the chicken directly over the flames and cook for 5 minutes until the skin is slightly charred and the internal temperature reads 165 degrees.
- Remove chicken from the heat and cut into pieces or halves.

SUPPERS

BBQ RIBS

SERVES: 6

What could be better than no fuss ribs? These babies bake slowly in the oven for several hours to get tender and juicy, then are thrown on the grill and slathered in bbq sauce to get that perfect sticky and sweet char. Instead of grilling, you can broil in the oven for 2-3 minutes each side.

INGREDIENTS

- 4 lbs baby back pork ribs
- 3/4 cups brown sugar
- 1 tablespoon fresh rosemary, minced
- 1 tablespoon paprika
- 1 tablespoon garlic powder
- 1/2 teaspoon cumin
- 1/2 teaspoon red pepper flakes
- 2 cups bbq sauce

DIRECTIONS

- Preheat the oven to 300 degrees and line a half sheet pan with aluminum foil.
- Pat each rib dry with a paper towel.
- In a small bowl, mix together the brown sugar, rosemary, paprika, garlic powder, cumin, and red pepper flakes. Spread rub mixture all over both sides of each rack of ribs.
- Wrap the ribs tightly with aluminum foil, crimping the edges and place on the sheet pan bone side up. Bake for 2 hours.
- Remove the aluminum foil from each rib and cut into serving portions, 2-3 ribs per portion.
- Slather each rib with the bbq sauce and grill for 2-3 minutes until slightly charred. Flip the ribs, apply more bbq sauce, and grill for another 2-3 minutes until slightly charred.

ADULT MAC & CHEESE

SERVES: 8

Everyone loves macaroni and cheese. I keep a box with the powdered cheese stocked at all times, but sometimes I want something my own age. This creamy mac and cheese is loaded with great flavors and fresh ingredients. This is the only "adulting" I want any part of!

INGREDIENTS

- 1 lb macaroni pasta
- 1 teaspoon salt
- 1 teaspoon black pepper
- 1 teaspoon garlic powder
- olive oil
- 3 cups portobello mushrooms
- 1 teaspoon fresh thyme, chopped
- 1 cup whole milk
- 2 tablespoons unsalted butter
- 2 cups sharp cheddar cheese, shredded
- 3/4 cup parmesan cheese plus more for topping, shredded
- 1 roma tomato, diced
- 1 cup panko bread crumbs
- fresh parsley, roughly chopped

DIRECTIONS

- Add the macaroni, salt, pepper, and garlic powder to a medium sized pot with water and cook according to the box's directions.
- While the macaroni is cooking, heat a sauté pan over medium heat and add 1-2 tablespoons of olive oil. Once the oil is hot, add the mushrooms and thyme and cook for about 8 minutes until the mushrooms are browned.
- Drain the macaroni and return to the pot. Add the milk, butter, cheddar cheese, and parmesan cheese and stir until melted. Stir in the mushrooms and tomatoes.
- Pour the macaroni mixture into a 9"x13" baking dish and add the panko bread crumbs over the top. Broil in the oven until the bread crumbs brown, about 2-3 minutes.
- Serve topped with parmesan cheese and parsley.

PAN SEARED SCALLOPS

SERVES: 4

This is a dish that definitely impresses. They can be served as an appetizer or as the main meal along with most sides. With their mildly sweet flavor and caramelized crust, they are the perfect classy meal.

INGREDIENTS

- 1 lb fresh bay or sea scallops
- 1 teaspoon black pepper
- 2 teaspoon fresh thyme, chopped
- 2 teaspoon garlic powder
- 4 tablespoons olive oil
- zest and juice from 1 lemon
- 1/2 cup dry white wine

DIRECTIONS

- Season scallops with the pepper, thyme, and garlic powder.
- Add olive oil to a large pan or skillet over medium-high heat. Once the oil is hot, add the scallops and sauté each side for 2 minutes until golden brown. Remove scallops from the pan.
- Using the same pan, add the white wine, lemon zest and juice, and scrape the browned bits from the bottom of the pan. Cook until the sauce is reduced by half, about 2-3 minutes.
- Pour the sauce over the scallops and serve immediately.

MAKE AHEAD TURKEY LASAGNA

SERVES: 8

I try and plan out my meals for the week so I'm nice and prepared, but that doesn't always happen. There are times when I know I'm going to have a crazy day and I won't feel like cooking, so I like to have one of these in the freezer to save the day. It's easy to prepare, and when it's ready to be cooked all there is to do is throw it in the oven and you'll have an amazing lasagna dinner ready in no time. Keep in the freezer for up to 3 months.

INGREDIENTS

- 1 lb ground turkey
- 1 lb turkey sausage
- 48 oz marinara sauce
- 4 cups mozzarella cheese, shredded
- 1 box oven-ready lasagna noodles

DIRECTIONS

- In a large pan or skillet, brown the ground turkey and turkey sausage. Drain and return to the pan off the heat. Stir in the marinara sauce.
- Spoon a small amount of the sauce into a disposable 9"x13" aluminum pan and spread around the bottom. Layer the lasagna by adding noodles, sauce, and cheese. Repeat for 2 more layers.
- Cover tightly with aluminum foil and place in the freezer. Transfer lasagna to the refrigerator 24 hours before cooking.
- When ready to cook, bake covered at 375 degrees for 1 hour.
- Remove aluminum foil, turn the temperature to 425 degrees, and bake for 10-15 minutes until the cheese is bubbly and slightly browned.

BEEF STEW

SERVES: 6-8

Classic cold weather comfort food. Tender meat and vegetables enveloped in a rich flavorful sauce.

INGREDIENTS

- 2 lbs boneless beef chuck roast, cubed
- 2 tablespoon vegetable oil
- salt and black pepper
- 3 garlic cloves, minced
- 1/3 cup red wine, such as merlot
- 7 cups beef stock
- 2 whole carrots, chopped
- 2 russet potatoes, peeled and cut into 1-inch cubes
- 1 medium onion, diced
- 1 tablespoon Worcestershire sauce
- 2-3 sprigs each of rosemary and thyme, tied together with kitchen twine
- 1/2 teaspoon red pepper flakes
- 1 tablespoon cornstarch

DIRECTIONS

- In a large stock pot or Dutch oven, add the vegetable oil over medium-high heat. Once the oil is hot, add the beef and season with 1 teaspoon of salt and 1 teaspoon black pepper.
- Cook 2-3 minutes until browned. Add the garlic and cook for 1 minute. Add the red wine, scraping up the browned bit at the bottom of the pan. Cook until the wine is reduced, about 3 minutes.
- Add the beef stock, potatoes, carrots, onion, Worcestershire sauce, rosemary and thyme bunch, red pepper flakes, and salt and black pepper to taste. Bring to a boil then reduce the heat to low, cover, and simmer for 30 minutes.
- Remove the lid and discard the rosemary and thyme bunch. Take out 1 cup of the liquid and whisk together with the cornstarch, then add back to the pot. Taste to see if any more salt is needed.
- Simmer uncovered for 5 minutes. Serve hot.

SUPPERS

SWEET & SPICY GRILLED CHICKEN BREAST WITH PINEAPPLE & MANGO SALSA

SERVES: 4

Chicken by itself is bland, boring, and tasteless, but with the right flavor you can turn chicken into something phenomenal. These tasty chicken breasts are grilled to perfection, slathered with a sticky honey and sriracha sauce and topped with a fresh pineapple and mango salsa. This dish smacks you will flavor from all directions!

INGREDIENTS

- 1/2 cup honey
- 4 tablespoons sriracha sauce
- 1 cup pineapple, diced
- 1 mango, diced
- 1/2 cup red onion, diced
- 1/2 cup bell pepper, diced
- 2-3 tablespoons fresh cilantro, chopped
- 4 boneless skinless chicken breasts
- salt and black pepper
- garlic powder
- juice from 1 lime

DIRECTIONS

- In a small bowl, whisk together the honey and sriracha sauce and set aside.
- Add the pineapple, mango, red onion, bell pepper, and cilantro to a medium sized bowl and stir to mix. Set aside.
- Season the chicken breasts with salt, pepper, and garlic powder to taste. Prepare the grill and oil the grate.
- When the grill is ready, add the breasts and cook for about 6-8 minutes each side. Brush the honey and sriracha sauce over the breasts, flip, and brush the other side.
- Serve hot topped with the pineapple and mango salsa and lime juice.

CHICKEN CASSEROLE

SERVES: 6-8

Chicken casserole is the ultimate comfort food! Something about the creaminess along with the toasted bread crumbs just makes you feel warm inside. This dish absolutely requires a nap afterwards!

INGREDIENTS

- 1 whole chicken
- 1 lemon, cut into 4 wedges
- 1 yellow onion, cut into 4 wedges
- 1 head garlic, cut in half lengthwise
- salt and black pepper
- 10-1/2 oz can cream of chicken soup
- 10-1/2 oz can cream of celery soup
- 2 cups chicken stock
- 4 cups herb stuffing
- 1 cup panko bread crumbs
- 1/2 cup (1 stick) unsalted butter, melted

DIRECTIONS

- To roast the chicken, preheat the oven to 425 degrees.
- Remove giblets from the inside of the chicken and pat dry with a paper towel. Add salt and pepper into the cavity then stuff with the lemon, onion, and garlic. Tie the legs together with kitchen twine and roast for 1-1/2 hours until the juices run clear.
- Let the chicken cool then debone and set aside.
- In a medium sauce pan, whisk the cream of chicken soup, cream of celery soup, and chicken stock over hight heat. Cook until the mixture is scalding hot (just before boiling). Remove from heat and set aside.
- Preheat the oven to 350 degrees.
- To assemble the casserole, layer half of the deboned chicken, half of the herb stuffing, and half of the soup mixture in a 9"x13" baking dish. Repeat for the second layer. Add the panko bread crumbs to the top and then pour the melted butter over the casserole. Cover with aluminum foil and bake for 30 minutes.
- Remove the foil and bake for 15 minutes. Turn the oven to broil and cook until the bread crumbs turn golden brown (it will only take a minute or so).

SUPPERS

CIDER BEER ROASTED CHICKEN

SERVES: 4

For this recipe, you'll need an infuser or roasting dish with a cylinder in the center. The infuser is filled with liquid that adds flavor by steaming the inside of the chicken while the outside roasts. You can infuse with any type of liquid, from beer, wine, to marinades. I love using cider beer in this dish. The aroma of the beer adds something special to the chicken, and as an added bonus, it makes the house smell amazing!

INGREDIENTS

- 1 whole chicken, 3-4 lbs
- 12 oz bottle cider beer
- 1 tablespoon salt
- 1 tablespoon black pepper
- 1 tablespoon fresh rosemary, chopped
- zest from 1 lemon
- olive oil

DIRECTIONS

- Preheat the oven to 425 degrees.
- Pour the beer into the infuser/cylinder of a chicken roaster.
- To prep the chicken, remove the innards and pat the chicken dry with a paper towel.
- In a small bowl, add the salt, pepper, rosemary, and lemon zest. Stir to combine. Add extra salt and pepper to the cavity. Rub the spice mix over the whole chicken and under the skin, being careful not to break the skin.
- Sit the chicken down onto the infuser. Brush the chicken all over with olive oil. Bake for 1 1/2 hours until the juices run clear when you run a knife between the leg and thigh and the internal temperature reads 165 degrees.
- Remove the chicken from the oven, wrap it with aluminum foil, and let rest for 15-20 minutes.
- Remove the chicken from the infuser and carve.

LINGUINE WITH ROASTED SHRIMP & CREAM SAUCE

SERVES: 4

This dish sounds more complicated than it really is. I've learned that roasting shrimp in the oven is an easy and tasty was to cook them. Simply prepare the pasta and sauce while the shrimp is roasting then toss everything together and you have a five star meal.

INGREDIENTS

- 1 lb shrimp, cleaned and deveined
- salt and black pepper
- 1 tablespoon fresh dill, chopped
- olive oil
- 1 lb linguine pasta
- zest from 1 lemon
- 2 cups heavy cream
- 2 cups fresh grated parmesan cheese plus more for topping
- fresh parsley, chopped

DIRECTIONS

- Preheat the oven to 400 degrees.
- Sprinkle shrimp with salt, pepper, and dill then toss in 1 tablespoon of olive oil. Spread the shrimp onto a sheet pan. Roast for 10 minutes until the shrimp are pink and firm.
- Bring a large pot of water to a boil. Add the linguine and 1 tablespoon of olive oil and cook according to the box's directions. Drain pasta, reserving 1/3 cup of the pasta water.
- In a large pan or skillet, cook the heavy cream until scalding (just before boiling) over medium-high heat.
- Remove from the heat and stir in 2 cups of parmesan cheese until melted. Add the linguine, lemon zest, and reserved pasta water and toss to coat with the sauce. Toss in the shrimp.
- Serve topped with parmesan cheese and parsley.

STUFFED BELL PEPPER CASSEROLE

SERVES: 8

My mom would fix this when I was a kid and it was my all time favorite! I would ask for it just about weekly. The savory meat and rice mixed with tons of mouthwatering cheese baked to perfection will be quickly added to your regular rotation. It's even better reheated the next day.

INGREDIENTS

- 2 lbs ground beef or turkey
- olive oil
- 1 medium onion, diced
- 1 teaspoon fresh thyme, chopped
- 2 garlic cloves, minced
- 1 bell pepper, diced
- 1 jalapeño pepper, chopped (seeded)
- 16 oz can diced tomatoes
- 1-1/2 cups white or basmati rice, uncooked
- 1 tablespoon Worcestershire sauce
- 1 tablespoon salt
- 2-1/2 cups beef stock
- 2 cups cheddar cheese, shredded
- fresh parsley, roughly chopped
- parmesan cheese, grated

DIRECTIONS

- Preheat the oven to 350 degrees.
- In a large pan or skillet, brown the ground meat, drain, and set aside.
- In the same pan, add 2 tablespoons of olive oil over medium heat. Add the onions and thyme and cook until the onions are soft and translucent, about 5 minutes. Add the garlic and cook for 1 minute. Add in the ground meat, bell pepper, jalapeño pepper, tomatoes, Worcestershire sauce, salt, beef stock, and rice. Cover with a lid and simmer for 15 minutes. Add shredded cheese and stir until melted.
- Transfer the mixture to a 9"x13" baking dish and cover with aluminum foil. Bake for 20 minutes, remove the foil, and bake for another 20 minutes.
- Serve hot topped with parsley and parmesan cheese.

SUPPERS

ROASTED TURKEY & GRAVY

SERVES: 10-12

I've always thought cooking a giant turkey to be very daunting and intimidating. Cooking a turkey is actually very easy. This roasted bird has flavor packed in every nook and cranny. After it's finished roasting, the flavor from the vegetables used to flavor the turkey are extracted to flavor the gravy. This ain't your grandma's Thanksgiving turkey!

SUPPERS

INGREDIENTS

- 1 whole turkey (10-12 lbs), giblets removed
- 1 whole head garlic, halved lengthwise
- 1 lemon, quartered
- 1 large onion, quartered
- rosemary & thyme sprigs, tied together with kitchen twine
- 2 cups (4 sticks) unsalted butter, room temp
- salt & black pepper
- 1 tablespoon fresh rosemary, chopped
- 1 tablespoon fresh thyme, chopped
- zest from 1 lemon
- olive oil
- 6-7 strips bacon
- juice from 1 lemon
- 1-2 rosemary sprigs
- 1 cup white wine
- 4 cups chicken stock
- 1/4 cup all-purpose flour

DIRECTIONS

- Preheat the oven to 350 degrees.
- Salt and pepper the inside of the turkey. Stuff the cavity of the turkey with the garlic, lemon quarters, onion quarters, and rosemary and thyme bunch. Tie the legs of the turkey together with kitchen twine. Place the turkey in a roasting pan breast side up.
- In a medium bowl, add the butter, 1 tablespoon salt, 1/2 tablespoon black pepper, chopped rosemary and thyme, and lemon zest and mash together with your hands until combined. Spread the butter mixture all over the turkey and between the skin and meat, being careful not to break the skin. Drizzle olive oil over the turkey and place the strips of bacon over the turkey.
- Bake for 2-1/2 to 3 hours, basting every 30 minutes until the internal temperature reads 165 degrees with an instant-read thermometer or the juices run clear when you cut between the leg and the thigh. Let the turkey rest for 30 minutes before carving.
- To make the gravy, add the pan drippings to a large pan or skillet over medium heat. Chop the bacon from the turkey and add to the pan. Remove the garlic, lemons, and onions from the cavity of the turkey, roughly chop, and add to the pan. Add the lemon juice and rosemary sprigs to the pan and sauté for 5 minutes. Add the white wine and cook until it's reduced by half, about 5 minutes. Add the chicken stock and simmer for 10 minutes.
- Strain the gravy through a sieve then add the gravy back to the pan, reserving 2 cups. Whisk the 2 cups of the reserved gravy with the flour, then add to the pan and simmer for 10 minutes. Serve warm with the turkey.

BAKED SALMON FILLETS WITH TOASTED PANKO

SERVES: 2

A simple easy-to-prepare meal with amazing elegant flavor.

INGREDIENTS

- 2 salmon fillets with skin on
- balsamic vinegar
- salt
- black pepper
- 2 tablespoons fresh dill, chopped
- zest and juice from 1 lemon
- 1 tablespoon olive oil
- 3/4 cups panko bread crumbs

DIRECTIONS

- Preheat the oven to 425 degrees. and line a sheet pan with parchment paper.
- Brush each fillet with balsamic vinegar. Sprinkle each fillet with salt, pepper, dill, and lemon zest. Add the fillets to the sheet pan with the skin side down and bake for 15-20 minutes until the internal temperature reads 140 degrees.
- While the fillets are baking, add the olive oil to a small sauce pan over medium heat. Once the oil is hot, add the panko bread crumbs and cook stirring constantly until the crumbs are browned, about 1-2 minutes.
- Once the fillets are done, sprinkle with panko crumbs and squeeze lemon juice over each fillet.

SUPPERS

MOROCCAN RISOTTO

SERVES: 4

Risotto is one of those fancy dishes that makes you feel...well fancy! Typically, Arborio rice is used in risottos; however, I like to use Orzo pasta which has more of a thicker bite to it. This rich and creamy one- pot meal will become an instant favorite.

INGREDIENTS

- 3-4 boneless chicken thighs, cut into bite-sized pieces
- salt and black pepper
- 1 tablespoon paprika
- 1 teaspoon ground ginger
- 1 tablespoon olive oil
- 6 cups chicken stock
- 6 tablespoon unsalted butter
- 1/2 cup onion, chopped
- 4 oz pancetta, cut into small cubes
- 8 oz portobello mushrooms, sliced
- 2 teaspoons fresh thyme, chopped
- 2 garlic cloves, minced
- 1-1/2 cup orzo pasta
- 1/2 cup white wine
- 1/2 teaspoon turmeric
- 3/4 cup fresh grated parmesan cheese plus more for topping
- fresh parsley, chopped

DIRECTIONS

- Add the chicken stock to a medium sized sauce pan and simmer over low heat.
- In a small bowl, mix together 1 tablespoon salt, 1/2 tablespoon pepper, paprika, and ground ginger. Season the chicken pieces with the spice mixture.
- In a Dutch oven, add the olive oil over medium-high heat. Once the oil is hot, add the chicken and cook for about 10 minutes until browned. Remove the chicken and set aside.
- Turn the heat down to medium and add the butter. Once melted, add the onions and pancetta and cook for 5 minutes. Add the mushrooms and thyme and cook for 3-4 minutes. Add the garlic and orzo pasta and stir to coat with the butter. Add the white wine, 1 teaspoon salt, 1/2 teaspoon pepper, and turmeric and cook until the wine is absorbed, about 2 minutes.
- Add 2 ladles of the chicken stock and cook until absorbed, stirring constantly. Repeat this step for 25 minutes until all the stock is used.
- Remove the Dutch oven from the heat and stir in 3/4 cup of parmesan cheese.
- Serve hot and topped with extra parmesan cheese and parsley.

ROASTED PEPPERS STUFFED WITH CAULIFLOWER RICE

SERVES: 6-8

I try to fix meals and dishes that are full of flavor but not calories. These stuffed peppers are a perfect low- carb meal that doesn't skimp on taste.

INGREDIENTS

- 1 head cauliflower, cut into small florets or 5-6 cups cauliflower rice
- olive oil
- 4 bell peppers
- 1/4 cup whole carrots, chopped
- 1/4 cup yellow onion, chopped
- 1 teaspoon fresh ginger, grated
- 1 tablespoon sesame seeds
- 1/2 teaspoon black pepper
- 1 garlic clove, minced
- 1 tablespoon rice vinegar
- 1 teaspoon sesame seed oil
- 1/4 cup low sodium soy sauce
- green onions, chopped
- juice from 1 lime

DIRECTIONS

- Preheat the oven to 425 degrees.
- Cut the tops off of the bell peppers, remove the seeds, cut in half lengthwise, and brush the outsides with olive oil. Set the bell pepper halves on a half sheet pan and set aside.
- Add the cauliflower florets to the bowl of a food processor and pulse until roughly ground. Work in batches as needed.
- Heat 1 tablespoon of olive oil in a large skillet or wok over medium-high heat. Add in the cauliflower rice, carrots, onions, ginger, sesame seeds, and pepper to taste. Sauté for about 5 minutes until the rice begins to soften. Add the garlic and cook for 1 minute. Add the rice vinegar, sesame seed oil, and soy sauce and stir to coat the rice. Remove from heat.
- Spoon the cauliflower rice into the bell pepper halves. Place the sheet pan in the oven and roast for 15 minutes until the cauliflower rice is slightly browned.
- Top each with green onions and lime juice.

SUPPERS

NEW ORLEANS STYLE GUMBO

SERVES: 6-8

If you've never been to New Orleans, you're really missing out. I love everything about the city, from the history to the culture, and most of all the food. Gumbo, which is the official cuisine of the state of Louisiana, is one of the many amazing dishes you'll find there. Gumbo isn't a quick fix meal. It's more of a lazy weekend meal that takes a while to make, but the pay off is definitely worth it!

SUPPERS

INGREDIENTS

- 1 lb boneless chicken thighs
- 1 lb smoked sausage, sliced into 1/2" pieces
- olive oil
- 1 medium onion, diced
- 1 bell pepper, diced
- 3 celery stalks, diced
- 6 garlic cloves, minced
- 1 jalapeño pepper, minced (seeded)
- 1/2 cup (1 stick) unsalted butter
- 1/2 cup all-purpose flour
- 1/2 cup white wine, such as sauvignon blanc
- 4 cups chicken stock
- 3 tablespoons Worcestershire sauce
- 14.5 oz can diced tomatoes
- 1 teaspoon fresh thyme, chopped
- 1 tablespoon Cajun or Creole seasoning
- 1 teaspoon salt
- 1 teaspoon black pepper
- 2 bay leaves
- 1 lb shrimp, peeled and deveined
- cooked white rice
- green onions, chopped
- fresh parsley, chopped

DIRECTIONS

- In a large pan or skillet over medium-high heat, add 2 tablespoons of olive oil. Once the oil is hot, add chicken thighs and sear each side for 3 minutes. Remove chicken, cut into 1" pieces, and set aside.
- Add the sausage to the pan and cook for 3-4 minutes until browned. Set aside.
- Add butter to a Dutch oven over medium-low heat. Once melted, add flour and whisk constantly for 20-30 minutes until the mixture turns dark brown or chocolate colored. Stir constantly so the mixture doesn't burn. Add onions, bell pepper, and celery to the Dutch oven and cook for 5 minutes until tender. Add the garlic and jalapeño and cook for 1 minute. Add the white wine and cook until absorbed, about 3 minutes.
- Slowly stir in the chicken stock and add the chicken, sausage, Worcestershire sauce, diced tomatoes, thyme, Cajun/Creole seasoning, salt, pepper, and bay leaves. Bring to a boil then reduce temperature to low, cover, and simmer for 2 hours stirring occasionally.
- Bring the heat up to medium and add the shrimp to the Dutch oven. Cook for 5 minutes until shrimp turns pink and slightly opaque. Remove and discard bay leaves. Skim any fat off the top with a spoon.
- Serve over rice topped with green onions and parsley.

SIDES

SIDES

SIDES

BROCCOLI CASSEROLE

SERVES: 6-8

A side dish that goes above and beyond the traditional mashed potatoes and peas. This cheesy creamy dish will become a new family favorite.

INGREDIENTS

- 8 cups broccoli florets
- 2 cups sharp cheddar cheese, shredded
- 1 cup mayonnaise
- 10.5 oz can cream of mushroom soup
- 2 eggs
- 1 teaspoon salt
- 1/2 teaspoon black pepper
- 2 cups panko bread crumbs
- 1/2 cup unsalted butter, melted

DIRECTIONS

- Preheat the oven to 350 degrees.
- Boil the broccoli in a large pot of water for 5 minutes, drain, and set aside to cool.
- In a large bowl, mix together the broccoli, cheese, mayonnaise, cream of mushroom soup, eggs, salt, and pepper until combined. Pour the mixture into a 9"x13" baking dish.
- In a small bowl, combine the panko bread crumbs and melted butter. Spread over the broccoli mixture.
- Bake for 30-35 minutes until the bread crumbs are browned.

SIDES

ROASTED BUTTERNUT SQUASH & CARROTS

SERVES: 4

I love to cook this earthy side in the fall when there's that snap of cold in the air. The butternut squash and carrots are tossed with subtle and simple flavors then roasted to perfection.

INGREDIENTS

- 1 butternut squash (2-3 lbs), peeled, seeded, and cut into 1" cubes
- 1-1/2 cups baby carrots
- 2 tablespoons fresh rosemary, chopped
- 1 teaspoon salt
- 1 teaspoon black pepper
- 3 tablespoons olive oil
- fresh parsley, chopped

DIRECTIONS

- Preheat the oven to 425 degrees.
- Add the butternut squash and carrots to a half sheet pan then toss with the rosemary, salt, pepper, and olive oil.
- Bake for 40-45 minutes until the butternut squash and carrots are tender and lightly browned.
- Top with parsley.

SIDES

SIDES

CORN OFF THE COB

MAKES: 4 cups

My parents make this side dish all the time and it's no wonder because it's over the top delicious. This dish requires very little ingredients since the flavor comes naturally from the corn.

INGREDIENTS

- 10 ears of corn, shucked and silks removed
- 2 tablespoons unsalted butter
- 1 teaspoon salt

DIRECTIONS

- Bring a large pot of water to a boil and add the ears of corn. Cook for 8-10 minutes.
- Plunge the finished corn into a large bowl filled with ice water to stop the cooking. Drain the water from the pot reserving 1/2 cup and set the pot aside.
- Over a large bowl, stand the corn cob upright and cut with a sharp paring knife down the length of the cob in a slow sawing motion about half the depth of the kernels. With the back of the knife scrape down the entire ear of the corn to remove the juices. Discard the cobs.
- Return the corn back to the pot over low heat. Add the butter, salt, and 2 tablespoons of the corn water. Cook for 10 minutes stirring constantly. If the corn begins to dry out, add more of the corn water 2 tablespoons at a time.
- Transfer the corn to a large heat proof bowl and serve.

SIDES

SWEET POTATO CRUNCH

SERVES: 6-8

This side always reminds me of the holidays. The sweet starchiness of the sweet potatoes topped with the crunch from the brown sugar and nuts are the perfect pairing with any holiday meal.

INGREDIENTS

- 4 lbs sweet potatoes, peeled and cut into 1" cubes
- 1/2 cup sugar
- 1 egg
- 1 teaspoon vanilla extract
- 1 teaspoon cinnamon
- 1/2 cup (1 stick) unsalted butter, melted
- 1/2 cup brown sugar
- 1/2 cup pecans, roughly chopped

DIRECTIONS

- Preheat the oven to 350 degrees.
- Add the sweet potatoes to a large pot of boiling water and cook until fork tender, about 15 minutes. Drain and allow the potatoes to cool slightly.
- Add the potatoes, sugar, egg, vanilla extract, and cinnamon to the bowl of a stand mixer fitted with the paddle attachment. Beat until smooth.
- Transfer the potato mixture to a 9"x13" baking dish and smooth out with a rubber spatula.
- In a separate small bowl, mix together the melted butter, brown sugar, and pecans until combined. Spread over top of the potato mixture.
- Bake for 35 minutes until the top is lightly browned.

STEVEN BAKER | www.StevenDoesFood.com

SIDES

GRILLED BACON WRAPPED ASPARAGUS

SERVES: 4

I've never been a big fan of asparagus, mainly because they've been served boiled or roasted with little to no flavor. These grilled asparagus, however, are tender, crunchy, and bursting with flavor.

INGREDIENTS

- 1 lb asparagus, trimmed
- 5-6 strips of bacon
- olive oil
- salt & black pepper
- garlic powder
- balsamic vinegar

DIRECTIONS

- Take 4 to 5 pieces of asparagus and wrap with a strip of bacon to secure in a bundle. Repeat with the remaining asparagus.
- Drizzle each bundle with olive oil then sprinkle with salt, pepper, and garlic powder to taste.
- Grill for 10 minutes with the lid on.
- Remove the bundles from the gill and drizzle with balsamic vinegar.

HERB ROASTED POTATOES

SERVES: 4

These are no basic run-of-the-mill potatoes.
The flavor volume gets turned way up with the fresh herbs and spices then roasted to crispy perfection.

INGREDIENTS

- 2 lbs Yukon Gold or red potatoes, cut into 1" cubes with skin on
- 1 medium onion, sliced
- 4 garlic cloves, minced
- 2 tablespoons fresh dill, chopped
- 1 teaspoon fresh tarragon, chopped
- 1-1/2 teaspoons ground mustard
- 1 teaspoon salt
- 1 teaspoon black pepper
- 4 tablespoons olive oil
- fresh parsley, chopped

DIRECTIONS

- Preheat the oven to 425 degrees.
- Add the potatoes and onion to a half sheet pan.
  Add the garlic, dill, tarragon, ground mustard, salt, pepper, and olive oil and toss to coat.
- Bake for 45 minutes stirring half way through until the potatoes are browned and crisp.
- Top with parsley.

SIDES

SIDES

MEXICAN RICE

SERVES: 4-6

Restaurant style Mexican rice made right at home, simple and easy.

INGREDIENTS

- 2 tablespoons canola oil
- 1/3 cup onion, chopped
- 4 garlic cloves, minced
- 2 cups long grain white rice
- 14.5 oz can crushed tomatoes
- 1 cup chicken stock
- 1 teaspoon salt
- 1/2 teaspoon cumin
- 1/2 teaspoon paprika
- 1/2 cup fresh cilantro, chopped and divided
- 1 roma tomato, diced
- juice from 1 lime

DIRECTIONS

- In a large sauce pan, heat the canola oil over medium heat. Once the oil is hot, add the onions and cook until soft and translucent, about 5 minutes. Add the garlic and cook for 1 minute.
- Add the rice and stir to coat with the oil. Stir in the can of crushed tomatoes, chicken stock, salt, cumin, paprika, and 1/4 cup of cilantro. Bring to a boil, reduce heat to low, cover, and simmer for 20 minutes.
- Remove from the heat and stir in the roma tomato, lime juice, and 1/4 cup cilantro.

SIDES

CAULIFLOWER FRIED RICE

SERVES: 4-6

A healthy alternative to traditional fried rice. All the flavor without all the calories!

INGREDIENTS

- 1 head cauliflower, cut into florets
- 2 eggs, beaten
- vegetable oil
- 3 garlic cloves, minced
- 1 tablespoon fresh ginger, grated
- 1 cup carrots and peas, fresh or frozen
- salt and black pepper
- 4-5 tablespoons soy sauce
- 1 tablespoon sesame seeds
- 1/4 teaspoon red pepper flakes
- 1 teaspoon rice vinegar
- 1 teaspoon sesame seed oil
- green onions, chopped

DIRECTIONS

- Add the cauliflower florets to the bowl of a food processor and pulse until roughly grated.
- Scramble the eggs and set aside.
- Add 3 tablespoons of vegetable oil to a large pan or wok over medium heat. Once the oil is hot, add the garlic and ginger and cook for 1 minute. Add the cauliflower rice, carrots and peas, soy sauce, red pepper flakes, sesame seeds, and a pinch of salt and black pepper. Cook stirring often until the cauliflower rice and vegetables are tender, about 10-15 minutes.
- Stir in the rice vinegar, sesame seed oil, and eggs. Add more soy sauce if needed.
- Top with green onions.

SIDES

CLASSIC THANKSGIVING DRESSING

SERVES: 8-10

Some of the best dishes and recipes are the ones that remind us of time spent with loved ones. This classic has been on the table every Thanksgiving of my life. Not only does it taste amazing, but it just gives you that warm comfort of home.

INGREDIENTS

- 4-5 cold Granddaddy's Southern Biscuits (pg 37)
- 4-5 cold Hoecakes (pg 40)
- 4 cups corn bread stuffing
- 4 hard boiled eggs, peeled and finely chopped
- 1 teaspoon salt
- 1 teaspoon black pepper
- 1 teaspoon fresh thyme, chopped
- 1/2 teaspoon ground sage
- 1/2 teaspoon poultry seasoning
- 4 cups chicken stock
- 1/4 cup (1/2 stick) unsalted butter

DIRECTIONS

- Add biscuits and Hoecakes to the bowl of a food processor and pulse several times for coarse crumbs.
- In a large bowl, mix together the biscuit and hoecake crumbs, corn bread stuffing, eggs, salt, pepper, thyme, sage, and poultry seasoning. Cover and refrigerate overnight.
- Preheat the oven to 350 degrees.
- Stir the chicken stock and melted butter into the mixture so that is it wet and moist. Dump the mixture into a 9"x13" baking dish.
- Bake for 15 minutes uncovered until the top is golden brown.

SIDES

POTATO SALAD

SERVES: 4-6

Every Easter my mom makes a juicy succulent ham with all the trimmings, including this timeless side. The tangy flavor of mustard with the sweet crunch of pickles makes this my favorite thing on the plate!

INGREDIENTS

- 8 cups chicken stock
- 5-6 russet potatoes, peeled and cubed
- 5 hard boiled eggs, peeled & finely chopped
- 1-1/4 cups mayonnaise
- 1/3 cup yellow mustard
- 1 teaspoon salt
- 1/2 teaspoon black pepper
- 3 tablespoons sweet pickle relish

DIRECTIONS

- In a large pot, add the chicken stock and 2 cups of water and bring to a boil. Add the potatoes and cook for 15 minutes until fork tender.
- Drain reserving 1/2 cup of the stock.
- Add the potatoes and 1/2 cup of the reserved stock to a large bowl and roughly mash with a potato masher. Stir in the eggs, mayonnaise, mustard, salt, pepper, and sweet pickle relish.
- Serve hot or cold.

MARINATED CARROTS

SERVES: 6-8

The perfect mixture of sweet and tangy and the best part is it can be made in advance.

INGREDIENTS

- 2 lbs whole carrots, peeled and sliced
- 1 large red onion, diced
- 1 bell pepper, diced
- 1 cup sugar
- 1/3 cup vegetable oil
- 3/4 cup apple cider vinegar
- 1 tablespoon fresh dill, chopped
- 5-6 basil leaves, chopped
- 1 teaspoon salt
- 1 teaspoon black pepper

DIRECTIONS

- Boil the carrots for 20 minutes until tender. Drain and set aside to cool.
- Combine all the ingredients in a large bowl. Cover and refrigerate overnight.

NAVY BEANS

SERVES: 4-6

The secret to these is time and patience. The beans soak all day to get that perfect texture then they simmer for several hours so all the flavors marry together. I don't use a lot of ingredients because the ham hock flavors the beans for me. It braises with the beans, releasing its natural salty flavor.

INGREDIENTS

- 1 lb dried navy beans
- 1/2 lb ham hock
- 2 teaspoons black pepper
- salt
- 6-7 strips cooked bacon, roughly chopped
- fresh parsley, roughly chopped

DIRECTIONS

- Rinse navy beans and place in a bowl with water. Cover and set at room temperature for 8 hours.
- Drain the beans and then add them to a large pot. Add 10 cups of water, the ham hock, and pepper to the pot. Bring to a boil, cover, and reduce the heat to low. Simmer for 2 hours.
- When done, taste to see if any salt is needed. Serve hot topped with bacon and parsley.

SIDES

SCALLOPED POTATOES

SERVES: 4-6

This side is served every time my family eats together. Nothing beats those cheesy tender potatoes with that wonderful crunch of bacon. These are the first thing I start off my meal with!

INGREDIENTS

- 2-1/2 to 3 lbs Yukon Gold potatoes, thinly sliced
- 2 garlic cloves, minced
- 2 teaspoons salt
- 1 teaspoon black pepper
- 4 tablespoons unsalted butter, cut into cubes
- 1 cup Colby Jack cheese, shredded
- 4-5 slices cooked bacon, roughly chopped
- fresh parsley, chopped

DIRECTIONS

- Preheat the oven to 350 degrees.
- In a 9"x9" baking dish, layer with half of the potatoes, 1 minced garlic clove, 1 teaspoon salt, 1/2 teaspoon pepper, and 2 tablespoons butter. Repeat for the second layer.
- Cover the dish with aluminum foil and bake for 1 hour and 15 minutes.
- Add the cheese and bacon and cover until the cheese melts. Top with parsley.

MASHED POTATOES

SERVES: 4

The very definition of comfort food. Forget these as a side dish, I could eat them as the entire meal!

INGREDIENTS

- 5-6 cups chicken stock
- 4 lbs russet or Yukon Gold potatoes, peeled and cut into 1" cubes
- 1 cup whole milk
- 4 tablespoons unsalted butter
- salt and black pepper
- fresh chives, chopped

DIRECTIONS

- Add the chicken stock to a large pot and bring to a boil.
  Add in the potatoes and cook until fork tender, about 15 minutes. Drain and return to the pot.
- In a small sauce pan, heat the milk and butter over medium heat until the butter is melted. Add the milk and butter mixture to the potatoes and mash with a potato masher until the potatoes are smooth and creamy. Add salt and pepper to taste. Top with chives.

SIDES

FRENCH FRIES

SERVES: 4-6

Fries are my addiction! If you think the only way to cook fries at home is to use frozen ones, then you're really missing out. Nothing beats homemade fries!

INGREDIENTS

- 5-6 large russet potatoes, rinsed
- 3 quarts vegetable oil
- table salt

DIRECTIONS

- Cut the ends off of each potato then cut the potato vertically into 4-5 pieces. Cut each piece into fries. Lay the fries on a paper towel and pat dry.
- Add the vegetable oil to a large pot or Dutch oven over high heat. Once the temperature of the oil reaches 360 degrees with a candy thermometer, carefully add the fries to the oil.
- Cook undisturbed for 20-25 minutes until the fires are golden brown. Remove the fries with a slotted spoon and place them on a sheet pan lined with paper towels.
- Immediately sprinkle with salt and serve hot.

DESSERTS

DESSERTS

BANANA PUDDING

SERVES: 6-8

There are two types of folks in the world, the ones that like cold banana pudding, and the ones that like it hot. The ones that like it hot are my people! Nothing beats that warm banana custard mixed with those crunchy vanilla wafers hot out of the oven. Heaven!

INGREDIENTS

- 3/4 cups sugar, divided
- 3 tablespoons all-purpose flour
- 1/4 teaspoon salt
- 3 eggs, separated
- 1 whole egg
- 2 cups whole milk
- 1 teaspoon vanilla extract
- 1/4 teaspoon cream of tartar
- 11 oz box vanilla wafers
- 4 ripe bananas, sliced

DIRECTIONS

- Preheat the oven to 375 degrees.
- Mix 1/2 cup of the sugar, flour, salt, 3 egg yolks, and 1 whole egg in a double boiler. Stir in the milk. With the heat on medium-low, stir constantly until the mixture thickens, about 8-10 minutes. Once the custard is the consistency of pudding, remove from the heat and stir in the vanilla extract. Set aside.
- To make the meringue, add the 3 egg whites, 1/4 cup sugar, and cream of tartar to the bowl of a stand mixer fitted with the whisk attachment. Beat until stiff peaks form.
- Add a small amount of custard to the bottom of a 10"x10" baking dish. Layer with half the vanilla wafers, 2 bananas, and half the custard. Repeat for the next layer then spread meringue over the top.
- Bake for 8-10 minutes until the meringue is browned.

STEVEN BAKER | www.StevenDoesFood.com

DESSERTS

CHEESECAKE

SERVES: 10-12

I make this cheesecake for Lake Gaston Coffee Company in Lake Gaston, North Carolina, and it's the most popular thing I make. The secret ingredient is Lake Gaston Coffee Company's very own coffee. You can't really tell it's there, but it brings out and accentuates all the other flavors. This is perfect to make in advance and freeze.

DESSERTS

INGREDIENTS

Crust:
- 2 cups graham cracker crumbs
- 2 tablespoons sugar
- 6 tablespoons unsalted butter, melted

Filling:
- 4 eggs, separated
- 1-1/2 cups sugar, divided
- 1/3 cup sour cream
- 2 teaspoons vanilla extract
- 3 tbsp (1 lemon) fresh squeezed lemon juice
- 1/3 cup brewed coffee, room temperature
- 2 tablespoons all-purpose flour, sifted
- 1/2 teaspoon salt
- 24 oz (3 blocks) cream cheese, room temp

DIRECTIONS

- Preheat the oven to 350 degrees and grease the bottom and sides of a 9-inch springform pan.
- For the crust, add the graham cracker crumbs and sugar to the pan and stir to combine. Stir in the melted butter until well incorporated. Press the crumb mixture evenly on the bottom and sides of the pan. Set in the refrigerator.
- In the bowl of a stand mixer fitted with the whisk attachment, beat the egg whites and 1/4 cup sugar until stiff peaks form. Remove the egg whites from the bowl and set aside.
- In the same bowl, beat the yolks for 1 minute. Mix in sour cream, vanilla extract, lemon juice, and coffee until well incorporated. Beat the remaining 1-1/4 cups sugar, flour, and salt until combined. Add cream cheese and beat until smooth. With a rubber spatula, gently fold in the egg whites until well mixed.
- Pour batter into the springform pan and smooth out the top. Lightly bang pan on the counter to remove air bubbles. Bake for 15 minutes, reduce heat to 200 degrees, then bake for 2 hours until center is firm.
- Turn off the oven and let the cheesecake sit for 3 hours. Remove from the oven and run a sharp knife along the inside edge of the pan to separate cake from the sides. Keep at room temperature for 1 hour.
- Refrigerate overnight before removing the cheesecake from the pan and slicing.

DESSERTS

PIE CRUST DOUGH

MAKES: 1 pie shell

The perfect foundation for a wide variety of sweet desserts as well as savory dishes.

INGREDIENTS

- 1-1/2 cups all-purpose flour
- 2 teaspoons sugar
- 1/4 teaspoon salt
- 2 tablespoons cold vegetable shortening
- 1/2 cup (1 stick) cold unsalted butter, cubed
- 4 tablespoons iced water

DIRECTIONS

- In the bowl of a food processor, add the flour, sugar, and salt and pulse several times to mix. Add the vegetable shortening and butter and pulse several times until the butter is the size of peas.
- With the processor on high, pour iced water down the feed tube until a ball of dough forms.
- Dump the dough onto a floured board and form a disc.
- Wrap the dough in plastic wrap and chill in the refrigerator for at least 30 minutes before rolling out.

DESSERTS

CHOCOLATE PIE

SERVES: 10-12

My grandmother would make these one night on our summer family vacation and it was the best night of the whole week! This dessert is decadent and rich but not overly sweet. The perfect end to any meal.

INGREDIENTS

- 1 unbaked pie crust dough (previous page)
- 1 cup sugar
- 3 tablespoons cocoa powder
- 1/3 cup cornstarch
- 2 egg yolks
- 3 egg whites
- 2 cups whole milk
- 1 teaspoon vanilla extract
- 2 tablespoons butter
- 1/2 teaspoon cream of tartar

DIRECTIONS

- Preheat the oven to 375 degrees.
- Roll out pie dough on a floured board 1" larger than the pie dish. Transfer the dough to the pie dish and cut off any excess dough around the edge. Crimp the edge with your fingers or a fork.
- Line the pie crust with buttered aluminum foil with the buttered side down. Fill the pie shell with pie weights or dried beans and bake for 20 minutes. When done, remove from the oven and discard the aluminum foil and pie weights. Set aside.
- In a medium bowl, add the sugar and sift together the cocoa powder and cornstarch. Set aside.
- Whisk together the egg yolks in a small bowl. Heat the milk to scalding (just before boiling) then remove from the heat and slowly stir in with the egg yolks.
- Add the egg mixture and dry ingredients together in a medium pot over medium-high heat. Whisk constantly until the mixture begins to thicken, about 5 minutes. Once it starts to thicken, stir with a spoon until it becomes the consistency of pudding. Remove from the heat and stir in the butter and vanilla extract. Pour the mixture into the pie crust.
- To make the meringue, whisk the egg whites and cream of tartar in the bowl of a stand mixer fitted with the whisk attachment on high speed until stiff peaks form. Spread the meringue over the pie filling and bake for 15-20 minutes until the meringue is browned.

LEMON POUND CAKE

SERVES: 12-16

I came up with the recipe by complete accident. I was attempting to make cake layers, but what came out of the oven wasn't the light cake I was aiming for. It was more dense, kind of like a pound cake. So I said, "What the hey, I'll just add tons of lemon flavor and see what happens." What came out was a rich, luscious pound cake with intense lemon flavor.

INGREDIENTS

Cake:
- 1 cup (2 sticks) unsalted butter, room temperature
- 2 cups sugar
- 3 cups cake flour
- 1 cup whole milk
- 1 teaspoon vanilla extract
- 1/2 teaspoon almond extract
- zest and juice from 2 lemons
- 3 eggs

Glaze:
- 1 cup confectioners' sugar
- 1/4 cup whole milk
- 1 tablespoon fresh squeezed lemon juice

DIRECTIONS

- Preheat the oven to 325 degrees and grease an 8"x4" loaf or bundt pan.
- In the bowl of a stand mixer fitted with the paddle attachment, beat the butter and sugar until creamy, about 2 minutes. Slowly mix in the cake flour until incorporated. Scrape the sides of the bowl if needed.
- Mix in the milk, vanilla extract, almond extract, and lemon zest and juice until well incorporated.
- Beat in eggs one at a time until combined.
- Spread the batter into the cake pan then bake for 1-1/2 hours until a toothpick comes out clean.
- Let the cake cool in the pan for about 15 minutes then remove from the pan and let cool on a wire rack.
- To make the glaze, in a small bowl whisk the confectioners' sugar, milk, and lemon juice until combined.
- Drizzle glaze over the cake.

DESSERTS

PUMPKIN CHEESECAKE

SERVES: 10-12

Cheesecake is usually my go-to dessert recipe and I'm always trying to find new versions to cook. Like a lot of other people, I go kind of pumpkin crazy in the fall, and this cheesecake fits in perfectly.

INGREDIENTS

Crust:
- 2 cups graham cracker crumbs
- 2 tablespoons sugar
- 1/2 teaspoon cinnamon
- 6 tablespoons unsalted butter, melted

Filling:
- 2 tablespoons all-purpose flour
- 1/2 teaspoon cinnamon
- 1/8 teaspoon nutmeg
- 1/8 teaspoon all spice
- 1/8 teaspoon ground ginger
- 4 eggs, separated
- 1-1/2 cups sugar, divided
- 1/3 cup sour cream
- 2 teaspoons vanilla extract
- 3 tablespoons (1 lemon) fresh squeezed lemon juice
- 1/2 teaspoon salt
- 15 oz can pumpkin puree
- 24 oz (3 blocks) cream cheese

DIRECTIONS

- Preheat the oven to 350 degrees and grease the bottom and sides of a 9" springform pan.
- For the crust, add the graham cracker crumbs, sugar, and cinnamon to the springform pan and stir to mix. Stir in the melted butter until well incorporated. Press the crumb mixture evenly on the bottom and sides of the pan. Set in the refrigerator.
- Over a small bowl, sift together the flour, cinnamon, nutmeg, all spice, and ginger and set aside.
- In the bowl of a stand mixer fitted with the whisk attachment, beat the egg whites and 1/4 cup sugar until stiff peaks form. Remove the egg whites from the bowl and set aside.
- In the same bowl, beat the egg yolks for 1 minute. Mix in the sour cream, lemon juice, and vanilla extract until well incorporated. Add the flour mixture, remaining 1-1/4 cups sugar, and salt and mix until combined. Add the cream cheese and pumpkin puree, then beat until smooth. With a rubber spatula, gently fold in the egg whites until combined.
- Pour batter into the springform pan and smooth out the top. Lightly bang pan on the counter to remove air bubbles. Bake for 15 minutes, reduce heat to 200 degrees, then bake for 2 hours until center is firm.
- Turn off the oven and let the cheesecake sit for 3 hours. Remove from the oven and run a sharp knife along the inside edge of the pan to separate cake from the sides. Keep at room temperature for 1 hour.
- Refrigerate overnight before removing the cheesecake from the pan and slicing.

STEVEN BAKER | www.StevenDoesFood.com

DESSERTS

OLD FASHIONED BUTTER CAKE WITH CHOCOLATE ICING

SERVES: 20-24

A southern dessert classic! Show up to a gathering with one of these and you are guaranteed to go home with an empty plate.

DESSERTS

INGREDIENTS

Cake Layers:
- 1-1/2 cups sugar
- 12 tablespoons unsalted butter, room temp
- 3 egg yolks
- 3 cups all-purpose flour
- 1 tablespoon baking powder
- 1 teaspoon salt
- 1 teaspoon vanilla extract
- 1-1/2 cups whole milk

Chocolate Icing:
- 1/2 cup cocoa powder
- 3 cups confectioners' sugar
- 1 cup (2 sticks) unsalted butter, room temperature
- 1 teaspoon vanilla extract
- 4 oz semi-sweet chocolate, melted and cooled
- 1/8 teaspoon salt
- 1/4 heavy cream

DIRECTIONS

- Preheat oven to 350 degrees and grease (3) 9" cake pans and line bottoms with parchment paper.
- In a medium bowl, add the flour, baking powder, and salt and stir with a fork to combine. Set aside.
- In the bowl of a stand mixer fitted with the paddle attachment, beat the sugar and butter together until creamed, about 1 minute. Mix in the egg yolks 1 at a time until well incorporated. Mix in vanilla extract. Slowly add flour mixture and milk a little at a time until well combined and batter is smooth.
- Evenly pour the batter into the cake pans and smooth out the tops. Bake for 20-25 minutes until a toothpick comes out clean. Remove the pans from the oven and let cool for 20 minutes then turn out on a wire rack to cool completely.
- For the icing, sift together the cocoa powder and confectioners' sugar and set aside.
- In the bowl of a stand mixer fitted with the whisk attachment, beat the butter until creamed, about 3-4 minutes. Mix in the vanilla extract, melted chocolate, and salt until well incorporated. With the mixer on low, slowly add the cocoa powder mixture and heavy cream a little at a time until well incorporated, stopping every so often to scrape down the sides of the bowl.
- Once well mixed, continue to beat on medium speed until smooth and creamy, about 2-3 minutes. Immediately apply to the cooled cake.

DESSERTS

MAMA LOU'S BUTTERSCOTCH PIE

SERVES: 10-12

This is my dad's favorite dessert and my grandmother's (everyone called her Mama Lou) recipe is over the top amazing. I rarely see butterscotch pie at restaurants and bakeries, and it's a real shame. It's rich, decadent, and delicious... pure pudding gold!

INGREDIENTS

- 1 unbaked pie crust dough (pg 94)
- 1/2 cup cornstarch
- 1-1/2 cups plus 2 tablespoons sugar, divided
- 3 eggs, separated
- 1/2 teaspoon maple flavoring
- 2 cups whole milk
- 2 tablespoons unsalted butter
- 1 tablespoon vanilla extract
- 1/4 teaspoon salt
- 1/4 teaspoon cream of tartar

DIRECTIONS

- Preheat the oven to 375 degrees.
- Roll out pie dough on a floured board 1" larger than the pie dish. Transfer the dough to the pie dish and cut off any excess dough around the edge. Crimp the edge with your fingers or a fork.
- Line the pie crust with buttered aluminum foil with the buttered side down. Fill the pie shell with pie weights or dried beans and bake for 20 minutes. When done, remove from the oven and discard aluminum foil and pie weights. Set aside.
- For the filling, in a medium-sized bowl, whisk together the cornstarch and 1-1/2 cups sugar to remove any lumps. Stir in the egg yolks, maple flavoring, and milk until combined.
- Add the mixture to a double boiler over medium-high heat. Whisk constantly until the mixture thickens to the consistency of pudding, about 10 minutes. Remove from the heat and stir in butter, vanilla extract, and salt. Pour mixture into the pie shell.
- For the meringue, beat egg whites, 2 tablespoons sugar, and cream of tartar until stiff peaks form. Spread over the pie filling.
- Bake for 10-15 minutes until the meringue turns golden brown.

DESSERTS

SWEET POTATO PIE

SERVES: 10-12

Picture it. It's Thanksgiving afternoon and you're stuffed with turkey and dressing, but you have just enough room for one more thing. Sweet potato pie is that thing! It's flavored with autumn spices and has just the right amount of sweetness. By the time you finish that slice, you'll be ready for that nap on the couch.

INGREDIENTS

- 1 unbaked pie crust dough (pg 94)
- 1 to 1-1/2lbs sweet potatoes (about 2 sweet potatoes), peeled and cubed
- 3 tablespoons unsalted butter, room temperature
- 3/4 cup buttermilk
- 2 eggs
- 1 cup brown sugar
- 1 tablespoon cinnamon
- 1/4 teaspoon nutmeg
- 1/4 teaspoon all spice

DIRECTIONS

- Roll out pie dough on a floured board 1" larger than the pie dish. Transfer dough to the pie dish and cut off any excess dough. Crimp the edge with your fingers or a fork. Set aside.
- Preheat the oven to 350 degrees.
- In a large pot, boil the sweet potatoes until fork tender, about 15 minutes. Drain, and set aside to cool.
- In the bowl of a stand mixer fitted with the paddle attachment, beat the sweet potatoes and butter until smooth. Add the buttermilk and mix until combined. Add the eggs one at a time until incorporated. Add the brown sugar, cinnamon, nutmeg, and all spice and mix until combined.
- Pour the batter into the pie shell and bake for 1 hour and 20 minutes until a toothpick comes out clean.

BROWNIES

SERVES: 10-12

Who doesn't love brownies? Rich, gooey, and packed with chocolate goodness. No wonder they're everyone's favorite dessert!

INGREDIENTS

- 1 cup all-purpose flour
- 1/4 cup cocoa powder
- 1 tablespoon baking powder
- 1/4 teaspoon salt
- 1/2 cup (1 stick) unsalted butter, melted
- 12oz semi-sweet baker's chocolate, roughly chopped
- 1 cup sugar
- 2 tablespoons brewed coffee
- 1 teaspoon vanilla extract
- 3 eggs

DIRECTIONS

- Preheat oven to 350 degrees and grease a 9"x13" baking dish.
- In a medium sized bowl, sift together the flour, cocoa powder, baking powder, and salt. Set aside.
- Add the butter and chocolate to a double boiler and cook until melted together and smooth.
- In a large bowl, stir together melted butter and chocolate with the sugar until combined. Stir in the coffee and vanilla extract. Once the mixture is slightly cooled, stir in eggs until combined. Stir the chocolate mixture with the flour mixture until combined.
- Pour and spread the batter into the baking dish and bake for 25-30 minutes until a toothpick comes out clean. Cool slightly before cutting.

DESSERTS

DESSERTS

CARROT CAKE

SERVES: 20-24

I think carrot cakes get a bad rep because people think they are difficult to make and take a lot of effort. Truth is, they aren't any harder than any other cake. You just get a good arm workout grating carrots!

INGREDIENTS

Cake Layers:
- 3 cups plus 1 tablespoon cake flour
- 2 teaspoons baking powder
- 2 teaspoons baking soda
- 2 teaspoons cinnamon
- 1/2 teaspoon salt
- 2 cups sugar
- 1 cup vegetable oil
- 4 eggs, room temperature
- 1 teaspoon vanilla extract
- 3 cups carrots, grated

Cream Cheese Icing:
- 1/2 cup (1 stick) unsalted butter, room temperature
- 8 oz cream cheese, room temperature
- 1 teaspoon vanilla extract
- 4 cups confectioners' sugar
- 1 cup walnuts, chopped

DIRECTIONS

- Preheat the oven to 350 degrees and grease (3) 9" cake pans lined with parchment paper.
- Sift together cake flour, baking powder, baking soda, cinnamon, and salt over a large bowl and set aside.
- Add the sugar, vegetable oil, eggs, and vanilla extract to the bowl of a stand mixer fitted with the paddle attachment and beat until combined, about 1 minute. With the mixer on low, slowly add the flour mixture a little at a time until well incorporated. Fold the grated carrots into the batter. Evenly pour the batter into the 3 cake pans.
- Bake for 30 minutes until a toothpick comes out clean. Set the pans aside for 10 minutes to cool, then turn the cakes over on a wire rack to cool completely.
- For the icing, beat the butter, cream cheese, and vanilla extract until creamed, about 3-4 minutes. With the mixer on low, slowly add the confectioners' sugar until combined. Fold in the walnuts.
- Make sure the cake layers are cooled completely before icing.

DESSERTS

PECAN PIE

SERVES: 10-12

A perfect combination of sweet & salty. Serve this southern classic warm with a scoop of vanilla ice cream.

INGREDIENTS

- 1 unbaked pie crust dough (pg 94)
- 3/4 cup sugar
- 1 cup light corn syrup
- 3 tablespoons unsalted butter
- 1/4 cup brown sugar
- 3 eggs
- 1 teaspoon vanilla extract
- 1 tablespoon bourbon
- 1/2 teaspoon salt
- 1/2 teaspoon cinnamon
- 1 1/2 cups pecans, roughly chopped

DIRECTIONS

- Pre-heat the oven to 350 degrees.
- Roll out the pie dough on a floured board 1" larger than the pie dish. Transfer the dough to the pie dish and cut off any excess dough around the edge. Crimp the edge with your fingers or a fork. Set aside.
- In a medium sauce pan, combine sugar and 1/2 cup water and bring to a boil. Cook until mixture starts to turn light brown then swirl the pan until the mixture turns golden brown. Turn down heat to medium and whisk in corn syrup until combined. Remove from heat and stir in butter until melted. Set aside.
- In a medium bowl, add the brown sugar, eggs, vanilla extract, bourbon, salt, and cinnamon and whisk to combine. Slowly whisk in the sugar mixture. Fold in the pecans.
- Pour the mixture into the pie shell and bake for 1 hour until the pie is slightly jiggly.

CARAMEL SAUCE

MAKES: 1-1/2 cups

A simple and sweet topping to almost any desert.

INGREDIENTS

- 3/4 cup sugar
- 1/3 cup water
- 3/4 cup heavy cream
- 2 tablespoons unsalted butter
- 1/4 teaspoon salt
- 2 teaspoons vanilla extract

DIRECTIONS

- Add the sugar to a medium sauce pan and pour in the water. Stir gently to moisten the sugar. Place the pan over high heat and leave undisturbed for 3-4 minutes until the mixture starts to caramelize.

- When you start to see color in the pan, gently swirl the pan in a circular motion so the mixture caramelizes evenly. When the mixture turns amber-brown, remove pan from the heat and slowly whisk in the heavy cream. Sauce will bubble up violently.

- Reduce the heat to medium and place the pan back on the heat. Continue to whisk until the sugar is no longer hard, about 2-3 minutes. Whisk in the butter, salt, and vanilla extract.

- Remove the pan from the heat and serve immediately or pour into an airtight container and refrigerate. When ready to use, place container in the microwave for 30 seconds until warmed.

KENTUCKY BOURBON CAKE WITH CARAMEL DRIZZLE

SERVES: 12-16

On a recent rip to Louisville, Kentucky, I discovered my love for bourbon. It's sweet yet smoky flavor is great to drink, but it's even better to cook with. This cake is sweet, rich, and scrumptious with an extra punch of bourbon in the caramel drizzle.

INGREDIENTS

Cake Layers:
- 2-1/2 cups cake flour
- 1 teaspoon baking powder
- 1/2 teaspoon baking soda
- 1/2 teaspoon salt
- 1/4 teaspoon nutmeg
- 1 cup (2 sticks) unsalted butter, room temperature
- 1-1/2 cups sugar
- 1/2 cup light brown sugar
- 3 eggs
- 1/2 cup buttermilk
- 1/4 cup bourbon

Caramel Drizzle:
- 1 cup sugar
- 1/3 cup water
- 2/3 cup heavy cream
- 1 tablespoon unsalted butter
- 1 teaspoon vanilla extract
- 2 teaspoons bourbon
- 3/4 cup pecans, chopped

DIRECTIONS

- Preheat oven to 350 degrees and grease and flour a bundt pan.
- In a large bowl, sift together the cake flour, baking powder, baking soda, salt, and nutmeg. Set aside.
- In the bowl of a stand mixer fitted with the paddle attachment, beat the butter until creamed, about 1 minute. Scrape the sides of the bowl with a rubber spatula.
- Mix in the sugar and brown sugar until combined. Add the eggs one at a time until incorporated. Add the flour mixture and buttermilk, alternating each, beginning and ending with the flour mixture. Scrape down the sides of the bowl and then mix in the bourbon.
- Pour the batter into the bundt pan. Bake for 40-45 minutes until a toothpick comes out clean. Allow the cake to cool for 15-20 minutes before removing from the pan.
- For the caramel drizzle, add the sugar and water to a sauce pan over high heat. Cook until the mixture begins to turn light brown, about 5 minutes. Once the color starts to change, begin to swirl the pan until the color changes to a dark brown. Whisk in the heavy cream until the sugar is completely dissolved (the mixture will bubble up violently).
- Remove the pan from the heat and stir in butter, vanilla extract, and bourbon. Drizzle caramel over the cake and top with pecans.

PUMPKIN OATMEAL COOKIES

MAKES: 20 cookies

Soft, fluffy cookies that are perfect for a fall dessert.

INGREDIENTS

- 2 cups all-purpose flour
- 1 teaspoon baking powder
- 1/2 teaspoon baking soda
- 1/2 teaspoon cinnamon
- 1/4 teaspoon nutmeg
- 1/4 teaspoon salt
- 3/4 cup (1-1/2 sticks) cold unsalted butter, diced
- 2 cups old fashioned oats
- 3/4 cup brown sugar
- 1/2 cup pumpkin puree
- 1/4 cup honey

DIRECTIONS

- Preheat the oven to 375 degrees and line a half sheet pan with parchment paper.
- Combine the flour, baking powder, baking soda, cinnamon, nutmeg, salt, and butter in the bowl of a food processor. Pulse several times until the butter is the size of peas.
- Transfer the flour mixture to a large bowl. Stir in the oats and brown sugar until combined. Stir in the pumpkin puree and honey until the dough begins to come together.
- Dump the dough onto a floured surface and knead until the dough forms. Roll the dough out to 1/2-inch thick and cut out each cookie with a biscuit or cookie cutter.
- Place the cookies on the sheet pan and bake for 10-15 minutes until golden brown.

CHOCOLATE SOUFFLÉ

SERVES: 6

I used to see the word "soufflé" in a cookbook, and I'd keep flipping the pages. I thought soufflés were hard to make, so I didn't even bother. It wasn't until I took a cooking class that I learned they are actually very easy. All it takes is a little preparedness. It's a delicious dessert and looks exquisite.

INGREDIENTS

Soufflé:
- 2-3 tablespoons unsalted butter, room temperature
- 1/2 cup sugar, plus more for dusting ramekins
- 8 oz semi-sweet chocolate, roughly chopped
- 3 tablespoons heavy cream
- 1 teaspoon vanilla extract
- 1/2 teaspoon instant espresso powder
- 6 eggs, separated
- 1/4 teaspoon salt
- 1/4 teaspoon cream of tartar

Whipped Topping:
- 1 cup heavy cream
- 1 tablespoon sugar
- 2 oz unsweetened chocolate, chopped

DIRECTIONS

- Preheat the oven to 350 degrees.
- Spread the butter on the bottom and sides of (6) 6 oz ramekins. Add about 1/2 tablespoon of sugar to each ramekin and swirl around to coat the entire bottom and sides. Dump out any excess sugar. Set ramekins aside.
- Add semi-sweet chocolate to a double boiler over medium heat. Once chocolate is melted, remove from the heat and stir in the heavy cream, vanilla extract, and espresso powder. Set aside.
- In the bowl of a stand mixer fitted with the paddle attachment, beat the egg yolks, 1/4 cup sugar, and salt until creamed, about 3 minutes. Slowly whisk in the chocolate mixture until combined.
- Clean the bowl of the stand mixer then add the egg whites, 1/4 cup sugar, and cream of tartar and beat on high speed with the whisk attachment until stiff peaks form. Fold in 1/3 of the egg whites into the chocolate mixture until well incorporated. Fold in the remaining egg whites.
- Evenly spoon the batter into each ramekin up to the inside rim. Lightly wipe the inside of the top of each ramekin to remove any batter. Place the ramekins on a sheet pan and bake for 15 minutes until the soufflé jiggles slightly.
- For the whipped topping, add the heavy cream and sugar to the bowl of the stand mixer fitted with the whisk attachment and beat until stiff peaks form. Fold in the chocolate. Add a dollop on top of each soufflé. Serve immediately.

THIS & THAT

THIS & THAT

BBQ SAUCE

MAKES: 4 cups

Seems like everyone has their own bbq sauce they make. There's a huge variety of flavors of bbq sauces. This one is sweet and tangy with a slight flare of heat. Great on any meat imaginable!

INGREDIENTS

- olive oil
- 5-6 garlic cloves, minced
- 2 cups ketchup
- 1/2 cup apple cider vinegar
- 1/3 cup molasses
- 2 tablespoons honey
- 1/4 cup brown sugar
- 2 tablespoons Worcestershire sauce
- 1/2 teaspoon black pepper
- 1 teaspoon red pepper flakes
- 1/2 teaspoon onion powder
- 1/4 teaspoon ground mustard

DIRECTIONS

- In a medium sauce pan, add 1-2 teaspoons of olive oil over medium heat. Once the oil is hot, add the garlic and cook for 1 minute then remove from the heat.
- Whisk in all the remaining ingredients, bring to a boil, reduce the heat to low, and simmer for 20 minutes stirring occasionally.

CANE & HERB DRESSING

MAKES: 2-1/4 cups

They used to serve this at a local restaurant that is unfortunately now closed. I fell in love with this dressing and once, while eating there, the waitress was awesome enough to give me the recipe. The sweet & tangy flavor topped off with fresh summer herbs makes this a perfect addition to any salad.

INGREDIENTS

- 1/2 cup fresh basil
- 1/4 cup fresh oregano
- 1/8 cup fresh thyme
- cloves from 1 head garlic
- 1/2 cup light corn syrup
- 1/2 cup molasses
- 1/4 cup spicy brown mustard
- 1/2 cup balsamic vinegar
- 1 teaspoon salt
- 1 teaspoon black pepper
- 3/4 cup olive oil

DIRECTIONS

- Add the basil, oregano, thyme, garlic, corn syrup, molasses, spicy brown mustard, balsamic vinegar, salt, and pepper to the bowl of a food processor. Pulse several times until pureed.
- With the food processor on high, pour the olive oil down the feed tube and process until emulsified.
- Refrigerate for up to 2 weeks.

SPICY HONEY MUSTARD

MAKES: 1-1/2 cups

Great to dip meat in or use as a sandwich spread.

INGREDIENTS

- 1 cup mayonnaise
- 1/4 cup yellow mustard
- 1 tablespoon Dijon mustard
- 1 tablespoon honey
- 1 teaspoon black pepper
- 1 teaspoon cayenne pepper
- 1 teaspoon fresh squeezed lemon juice

DIRECTIONS

- Whisk all ingredients together and refrigerate. Keeps for up to 5 days.

STRAWBERRY VINAIGRETTE

MAKES: 2 cups

This vinaigrette is quick and simple to make and it goes great on any salad. The summertime fresh, tangy, and tart strawberries sends the flavor right over the edge!

INGREDIENTS

- 1 pint fresh strawberries, washed with tops cut off
- 2 tablespoons balsamic vinegar
- 1 tablespoon honey
- 1/4 teaspoon salt
- 1/4 teaspoon black pepper
- 1/4 cup olive oil
- 1 tablespoon poppy seeds

DIRECTIONS

- Add the strawberries, balsamic vinegar, honey, salt, and pepper to the bowl of a food processor.
- With the food processor on high, pour the olive oil down the feed tube and process until emulsified.
- Stir in the poppy seeds.

CREAMY GREEK YOGURT DRESSING

MAKES: 2 cups

This light and creamy dressing is great on just about anything.

INGREDIENTS

- 1 cup plain Greek yogurt
- 1 tablespoon fresh dill, chopped
- 1-1/2 tablespoons fresh chives, chopped
- 1/2 tablespoon fresh parsley, chopped
- 1 garlic clove, minced
- 2 tablespoons fresh squeezed lemon juice
- 2 tablespoons white wine vinegar
- 1/2 teaspoon salt
- 1/4 teaspoon black pepper
- 1/4 cup olive oil

DIRECTIONS

- In a large bowl, whisk all ingredients together until combined.

THIS & THAT

CLASSIC MARGARITA

MAKES: 2 drinks

Margarita. Best drink ever. Nuff said.

INGREDIENTS

- 4oz tequila
- 2oz orange liqueur
- 3oz fresh squeezed lime juice
- 1oz simple syrup
- kosher salt
- lime wedges for garnish

DIRECTIONS

- Pour the tequila, orange liqueur, lime juice, and simple syrup in a beverage shaker with ice and shake for 30 seconds.
- Strain in glasses over ice, rim with kosher salt and garnish with lime wedges.

ORANGEADE

MAKES: 2 drinks

When I was a kid, my mom would take my little sister and I to a local soda fountain for these. It gave me something to look forward to all day! This fresh & vibrant drink will be a favorite for all.

INGREDIENTS

- 2 cups fresh squeezed orange juice (5-6 oranges)
- 1-1/2 cups simple syrup
- maraschino cherries

DIRECTIONS

- In a small pitcher, stir together the orange juice and simple syrup.
- Pour in glasses over ice topped with maraschino cherries.

THIS & THAT

PITCHER OF MARGARITAS (FOR CHEATERS)

MAKES 3 liters

Margaritas should really be made with freshly squeezed lime juice, but when making a pitcher of them, who wants to squeeze that many limes?! Thank goodness for good margarita mix! Just quickly mix all the ingredients together and you're ready for a party!

INGREDIENTS

- 3 cups tequila
- 2 cups orange liqueur
- 8 cups margarita mix, such as Jose Cuervo
- sliced limes for garnish
- kosher salt

DIRECTIONS

- In a large pitcher, mix together the tequila, orange liqueur, and margarita mix. Cover and chill.
- Serve in chilled glasses rimmed with kosher salt. Garnish with lime wedges.

SIMPLE SYRUP

MAKES: 1 cup

INGREDIENTS

- 1 cup sugar
- 1 cup water

DIRECTIONS

- In a medium sauce pan, combine the sugar and water and bring to a boil. Cook until the sugar is dissolved.
- Remove from the heat and set aside to cool.
- Store in an air tight container for up to 1 month.

GROWN-UP LEMONADE

MAKES: 2 drinks

This sweet and tart beverage fits right in on a hot summer day by the pool.
You can of course leave out the vodka, but why would anyone want to do a crazy thing like that?!

INGREDIENTS

- 2 cups fresh squeezed lemon juice (about 8 lemons)
- 1 cup simple syrup (pg 116)
- 3/4 cup vodka
- sugar

DIRECTIONS

- In a small pitcher, stir together the lemon juice, simple syrup, and vodka.
- Serve in chilled glasses rimmed with sugar.

MOJITO

MAKES: 1 drink

This refreshingly cool drink is perfect on a hot summer day. **Just a word to the wise:**
mix in the club soda AFTER you shake the drink or you'll get explosive results. I know from experience!

INGREDIENTS

- 3/4 cup light rum
- 1/4 cup fresh squeezed lime juice
- 1-1/2 tablespoons sugar
- 12 mint leaves plus more for garnish, roughly torn
- club soda

DIRECTIONS

- Add the rum, lime juice, sugar, mint leaves, and ice to a beverage shaker and shake for 30 seconds.
- Pour into glass over ice and top off with a splash of club soda.
- Garnish with mint leaves and lime wedges.

THIS & THAT

MARINARA SAUCE

MAKES: 2 quarts

Store-bought marinara sauce is fine, there are some great ones out there, but there's nothing like making your own from scratch. I like to make big batches and can them so I always have some on hand.

INGREDIENTS

- 1 medium onion, diced
- 2 whole carrots, diced
- olive oil
- 7-8 garlic cloves, minced
- (2) 28 oz cans crushed tomatoes
- 5-6 fresh basil leaves, chopped
- 1 tablespoon oregano
- 2 teaspoons salt
- 1 teaspoon black pepper
- 2 bay leaves

DIRECTIONS

- In a large pot or Dutch oven, add 1-2 tablespoons of olive oil over medium heat. Once the oil is hot, add the onions and carrots and cook until tender, about 5 minutes.
- Add the garlic and cook for 1 minute. Add the crushed tomatoes, basil, oregano, salt, pepper, and bay leaves.
- Cover and simmer lover low heat for 45 minutes, stirring occasionally.
- To smooth out the sauce, blend with an immersion blender or in batches in a blender or food processor.

STICKY & SWEET BOURBON SAUCE

MAKES: 2 cups

A sauce perfect for dipping and grilling any variety of meat. Get extra napkins ready... you'll need them!

INGREDIENTS

- 1/4 cup bourbon
- 1 cup pineapple juice
- 2 tablespoons teriyaki sauce
- 2 tablespoons soy sauce
- juice from 1 lemon
- 6 garlic cloves, minced
- olive oil
- 1/4 cup honey
- 1 cup dark brown sugar
- 1 tablespoon onion powder
- 1/2 tablespoon red pepper flakes
- 2 tablespoons corn starch

DIRECTIONS

- In a small bowl, stir together the bourbon, pineapple juice, teriyaki sauce, soy sauce, and lemon juice and set aside.
- Add 1 tablespoon of olive oil to a medium sauce pan over medium heat. Once the oil is hot, add the garlic and cook for 1 minute. Stir in the bourbon mixture and remove from the heat.
- Whisk in the honey, brown sugar, onion powder, and red pepper flakes. Bring to a boil then reduce the heat to low and simmer for 1 hour, stirring occasionally.
- In a small bowl, whisk together the cornstarch and 2 tablespoons of hot water. Add to the sauce and whisk until incorporated and the sauce thickens. Remove from heat.

THIS & THAT

KITCHEN CONVERSIONS

INGREDIENT SUBSTITUTIONS

ORIGINAL	SUBSTITUTE
almond extract (1/2 tsp)	vanilla extract (3/4 tsp)
baking powder (1 tsp)	1/4 tsp baking soda + 1/2 tsp cream of tartar
buttermilk (1 cup)	1 tbsp lemon juice or vinegar + enough milk for 1 cup
chocolate, semi-sweet (~1/3 cup)	3 tbsp unsweet cocoa pwdr + 1-1/2 tbsp granulated sugar + 1-1/2 tsp butter oil
corn syrup (1 cup)	1-1/4 cup granulated sugar, dissolve in 1/4 cup hot water
Italian seasoning (2 tsp)	1 tsp dried oregano + 1/2 tsp dried basil + 1/2 tsp dried thyme
pumpkin pie spice (1 tsp)	1/2 tsp cinnamon + 1/4 tsp gnd nutmeg + 1/4 tsp gnd ginger + 1/2 tsp gnd cloves
sugar, dark brown (1 cup)	1 cup granulated sugar + 2 to 3 tbsp molasses
sugar, light brown (1 cup)	1 cup granulated sugar + 1 to 2 tbsp molasses
sugar, powdered (~1 cup)	1/2 cup + 1-1/2 tbsp granulated sugar + 3/4 tsp corn starch, finely ground in blender
tomato paste (1 tbsp)	2 to 3 tbsp tomato purée or tomato sauce, boil to 1 tbsp
vanilla bean (8" pod)	2 to 3 tsp vanilla extract

SPOONS & CUPS

TEASPOONS	TABLESPOONS	CUPS
3 tsp	1 tbsp	1/16 cup
6 tsp	2 tbsp	1/8 cup
12 tsp	4 tbsp	1/4 cup
18 tsp	6 tbsp	1/3 cup
24 tsp	8 tbsp	1/2 cup
36 tsp	12 tbsp	3/4 cup
48 tsp	16 tbsp	1 cup

LIQUID EQUIVALENTS

1 cup	8 ounces
1 pint	2 cups / 16 ounces
1 quart	4 cups / 32 ounces
1 gallon	4 quarts / 128 ounces

TEMPERATURE

FAHRENHEIT	CELSIUS
250° F	121° C
300° F	149° C
325° F	163° C
350° F	177° C
375° F	190° C
400° F	204° C
425° F	218° C
450° F	232° C
475° F	246° C
500° F	260° C

www.ingramcontent.com/pod-product-compliance
Lightning Source LLC
Chambersburg PA
CBHW061757290426
44109CB00030B/2881